FINDING MOTHER

A JOURNEY OF LOSS AND LOVE

AN ANTHOLOGY OF THE
FINDING MOTHER SERIES
OF FOUR CHRONOLOGICAL MEMOIRS

Dr. Grace LaJoy Henderson

Inspirations by Grace LaJoy
Raymore, MO 64083

Finding Mother: A Journey of Loss and Love

Disclaimer. I have tried to recreate events, locales and conversations from my memories of them. In order to maintain their anonymity in some instances I have changed the names of individuals and places. I may have changed some identifying characteristics and details such as physical properties, occupations and places of residence.

Due to the delicate subject of mental illness, all names are fictitious. I have taken great precaution to ensure my mother could not be located, while still sharing my real-life story.

Mission. Sharing my story to help increase awareness of mental illness.

Goal. Reducing stigma. Fostering connection. Inspiring hope.

Finding Mother: A Journey of Loss and Love
Copyright 2020. Grace LaJoy Henderson
Written by Grace LaJoy Henderson
Published by Inspirations by Grace LaJoy
Raymore, MO 64083

ISBN: 978-1-7341868-7-1

All rights reserved. No portion of this book may be reproduced, photocopied, stored or transmitted in any form except by prior written approval of the publisher.

Printed in the United States of America

Acknowledgement

The *Finding Mother Series* is my own recollection of my siblings' and my reunion with our mother after forty-nine years. When referring to my father, mother and siblings, I use fictitious names, as this is *my* story to tell. Their accounts may be different, as they may have perceived things from a different angle.

About the Series

The *Finding Mother Series* is a complex, touching opportunity for readers to see into the author's journey to find her mother after decades. This series would be ideal for students at a secondary level who are searching for insight about the emotional conflicts and battles one must face when someone they care about has a mental illness. The four books in the series are segmented to provide specific lenses to the overall process, with a number of opportunities available for opening discussions about mental illness from both the author's point of view and her mother's. **~Leslie Arambula, MA Creative Writing, English Teacher**

A WORD FROM THE AUTHOR
ABOUT THE FINDING MOTHER SERIES

Stories like mine are common and there is a sincere need to establish dialogue concerning this issue.

When I asked my mother how she felt about me publishing our reunion story, she laughed and said, "I guess it will be alright." Then she laughed again. She seemed flattered. Therefore, I really want her to feel proud about the way I present my recollection of the story. I told her I would not be revealing her real name or location.

To protect my mother's privacy, I have not revealed the full name under which she was found. I would never have found her under the name listed in my original foster care storybook. I believe that my personal recollection of our reunion details will inspire you. I hope it will decrease the stigma of mental illness in order to promote helpful discussion about this subject.

Due to my own personal struggle with the stigma surrounding mental illness, initially, I was only going to share the positive details of finding and reuniting with my mother. I did not intend to share any of the parts that were embarrassing for me. However, when others heard my story of how I found my mother after five decades, they told me they felt inspired. Many had similar stories. Realizing my personal story was intriguing, and could be helpful to so many people, I am sharing it…all of it.

TABLE OF CONTENTS

**BOOK ONE - FINDING MOTHER AFTER FIVE DECADES :
A STORY OF HOPE**

FOREWORD – DR. THERESA TORRES, PROFESSOR OF SOCIOLOGY
PREFACE
INTRODUCTION
CHAPTER 1 - BEFORE MOTHER LEFT
CHAPTER 2 - AFTER MOTHER LEFT
CHAPTER 3 - THE SEARCH
CHAPTER 4 - THE SEARCH CONTINUES
CHAPTER 5 - STILL SEARCHING
CHAPTER 6 - LOSING HOPE, THEN FINDING A GLIMMER
CHAPTER 7 - I FOUND MY MOTHER!

**BOOK TWO – REUNITING WITH MOTHER:
A STORY OF TENACITY**

FOREWORD – JACOB KELOW, SECONDARY SCHOOL COUNSELOR
PREFACE
INTRODUCTION
CHAPTER 1 - AFTER FINDING MOTHER
CHAPTER 2 – SEEING MOTHER AFTER 49 YEARS
CHAPTER 3 – WILL MOTHER ACCEPT US?
CHAPTER 4 – REUNITED
CHAPTER 5 – OUR FINAL VISIT WITH MOTHER

BOOK THREE – AFTER THE REUNION:
A STORY OF ACCEPTANCE

FOREWORD – ARICA MILLER, LMSW
INTRODUCTION
CHAPTER 1 - RETURNING HOME AFTER THE REUNION
CHAPTER 2 - MY SEARCH FOR A PLACE FOR MOTHER
CHAPTER 3 - A TYPICAL PHONE CALL WITH MOTHER
CHAPTER 4 - MY SECOND TRIP TO VISIT MOTHER
CHAPTER 5 - ARRIVING ON THURSDAY EVENING
CHAPTER 6 - DAY TWO OF OUR VISIT – FRIDAY
CHAPTER 7 - DAY TWO OF OUR VISIT – TALKING WITH MOTHER
CHAPTER 8 - DAY TWO OF OUR VISIT – TALK ABOUT MOVING
CHAPTER 9 - DAY THREE OF OUR VISIT – SATURDAY
CHAPTER 10 - DAY FOUR OF OUR VISIT – SUNDAY
CHAPTER 11 - DAY FOUR OF OUR VISIT – WHY MOTHER LEFT
CHAPTER 12 - DAY FOUR OF OUR VISIT – RETURNING HOME

BOOK FOUR – DIARY OF EMOTIONS:
THOUGHTS AND FEELINGS

FOREWORD – PHYLLIS HARRIS, FORMER MISSOURI DIRECTOR
FOREWORD – JACOB KELOW, SECONDARY SCHOOL COUNSELOR
PREFACE
INTRODUCTION
AFTER MY SECOND TRIP
July 20, 2018
August 11, 2018
August 11, 2018 – Addendum
August 12, 2018
August 22, 2018
August 22, 2018
September 9, 2018
September 12, 2018
September 15, 2018

Finding Mother: A Journey of Loss and Love

September 16, 2018
September 17, 2018
September 30, 2018
October 5, 2018
October 6, 2018
October 8, 2018
October 26, 2018
November 1, 2018
November 20, 2018
November 22, 2018
December 1, 2018
January 23, 2019
January 23, 2019
April 20, 2019
April 28, 2019
May 12, 2019
May 13, 2019
June 16, 2019
August 6, 2019
September 15, 2019
September 22, 2019
September 24, 2019
IN CLOSING

FOR EACH BOOK
DISCUSSION QUESTIONS
QUESTIONS TEACHERS CAN ASK
FURTHER DISCUSSION POINTS
FINDING MOTHER SERIES
ABOUT THE AUTHOR

Finding Mother: A Journey of Loss and Love

Book One

Finding Mother after Five Decades: A Story of Hope

DEDICATION

To "April" for answering a phone and confirming that my journey in searching for my mother had come to an end. I have finally found her.

To my brother "Jerome", the first person I called when I suspected I might have located Geneva. You did some footwork of your own and helped confirm that the person I had come across was indeed our mother.

Foreword

A powerful, gripping read! *Finding Mother After Five Decades* is the emotional journey of the author to locate her mother who abandoned her when she was only two years old. This book held my attention and kept me wanting to know why her mother left and where she went. As the author unraveled the impact of mental illness on her mother's life, I felt compassion for the author, her mother, and siblings. This captivating book left me eager to read the next book in the *Finding Mother Series*.

Reading this story also offers hope to people in search of their parents.

~ **Dr. Theresa Torres, Professor of Sociology**
University of Missouri–Kansas City

PREFACE

When I estimated that my mother would be close to eighty years old, I nearly gave up all hope that I might see her again. *In Finding Mother after Five Decades*, I share specific details about my tedious journey of searching unsuccessfully, giving up, then finally finding my mother after forty-nine years.

INTRODUCTION

When my mother left in 1969, I was two years old, and when I finally found her in 2018, I was fifty-one years old.

Forty-nine years, that is how long it took me to see her face again. However, I like to refer to the timing as five decades because it was so close to the fifty-year mark.

This worn out folder represents every effort, challenge, and failure I endured in my very long and tedious search for my long-lost mother until the final success of reuniting with her. In this folder are birth certificates, birth records, marriage record requests, private detective reports, letters I sent, social security information, and the list goes on.

I finally found my mother on March 2, 2018. Just over a year later, on July 1, 2019, I began sorting through these items, placing them in chronological order, so that I could eventually lay out for you every hardship and obstacle I had to overcome in order to hug my mother one more time.

My first recollection of my mother was when I was two. I was too little to realize fully what was going on, but I vividly remember the day she left my siblings and me in the care of our father.

Over the years, this lack of motherly care was something that was constantly on my mind. Whenever I had the chance, I tried to get as much information as I could from my father, the person who knew her better than anyone.

When I finally came of age, it took me thirty-three years to find the mother I was yearning for.

Even as I was filling this folder up, I never truly believed the day would come when I would actually see my mother again.

Now, it feels amazing to be telling the world how I have finally found her when, more than once, my hopes were crushed and I thought it would never happen for me.

Chapter 1
BEFORE MOTHER LEFT

She has to be somewhere! That is what I used to exclaim, frustrated when my mother seemed to have vanished into thin air and all of my search efforts were coming up null.

Why did she have to leave?

Why *my* mother?

Why do I have to endure such a devastating heartache?

Most importantly, why can't I find her?

Those were the thoughts and questions that lingered in my mind over the years, as the trail of my mother's whereabouts was getting colder with each passing day.

Even though I was only two years old when she left in 1969, I can recall with vivid details of numerous events that took place at that time.

One of the most heartbreaking memories I have is this one: My mother picking me up in her arms and walking out of the back door of our rental house. She walked, across the very tall, uncut grass to the back area of the lawn, lay face down in the grass and cried her heart out. I lay beside her and cried with her. At the time, I did not understand why she was so miserable that she would sob so heavily in front of her little girl.

I only remember feeling heartbroken for her.

I felt her pain so very deeply.

It was like her pain was my pain and I hurt terribly for her that day.

I later learned that my father had called the authorities to have her picked up and taken, against her will, to a mental hospital.

So, during that moment of weeping in the grass, she knew she was about to be separated from her family.

Finding Mother: A Journey of Loss and Love

It seemed as though my father had been insensitive to his wife's illness. But, I guess if she was posing a threat to herself and others, my father may have felt he was doing something good.

Here is a less heartbreaking, yet deeply hurtful, memory: I was in the car with my family, when my father and mother began to argue. I was no more than one or two years old, but I remember feeling like my father's voice was loud and abusive and my mother was quiet and hurt from the dispute.

It felt like the argument was not fair because my father was louder, stronger, and angrier, while my mother seemed weak and unable to defend herself.

During this particular quarrel, my mother took me in her arms, got out of the car, slammed the door, and walked away with me. I do not remember if my father had demanded her to get out or if it was her choice. I only remember her getting out of the car.

While I do not recall anything that happened after that, my oldest sister, Carla often expressed her surprise about how my mother and I made it home before *they* did even though they were in the car and my mother had left walking.

When I really look back, my time with my mother was a painful one. Although I have always remembered both good and bad, the bad was ugly. I heard stories about my mother's mental illness causing her to experience episodes, which resulted in her harming my siblings and me. Overall, my father and mother had a strained relationship. They both endured an enormous amount of pain, resulting in the breakup of our family.

Growing up, I blamed my father for my mother's emotional state. I felt like his physical abuse caused her to leave us.

Over the years, my brother Jerome tried to explain to me that our mother really *did* have a serious mental illness and our father was not to blame for that.

"You don't understand, Grace. Our mother was not the sane person you think she was," Jerome used to say.

Finding Mother: A Journey of Loss and Love

He remembered it better than *I* did because he was the oldest of the six children and I was the baby. He explained to me that my father usually physically harmed her because she physically harmed us.

Although I continued to blame my father, I *do* recall an instance where I know it to be true. My father came home from work one evening to find bruises on me. Mother had beaten me with a broomstick. In turn, he gave her a beating with the same broomstick. Not understanding the concept of revenge, I felt a deep sadness for the lady who gave birth to me. This is the only time I remember my mother hurting me, but not the only time I witnessed my father hitting her.

I never believed that my poor mother deserved to be abused regardless of the circumstances.

Right or wrong, that was just how I felt whenever I would think back about my parents' relationship. I guess my father was trying to protect us the only way he knew at the time. But, the way he went about it was very wrong in my eyes.

She was not mentally able to care for a family of eight.

My grandmother stepped in to help when she could, but I believe this still caused a major hardship for my father; they had six children, and he was carrying the entire family financially without any support from his wife.

I believe my father experienced a lot of stress and disappointment due to my mother having a mental illness and not being able to provide him with the support he desired from a wife. She was unable to work, cook meals, or clean the house the way my father expected her to.

Then, to come home after a very long, tedious work day and find no dinner ready, the house dirty, or her having harmed one of the children, was an even heavier burden.

I imagine this had to be difficult for both of my parents as they were living in an era where the wife was naturally expected to perform the duties of the household while the husband worked.

Chapter 2
AFTER MOTHER LEFT

After my mother left, my father seemed very angry with her for not fulfilling his expectations. I do not believe he truly understood that she was not capable of being the person he needed her to be.

I believe he sincerely felt like he could just "knock some sense into her" and he tried his hardest so many times to do just that…unsuccessfully.

But, it is weird because even with all of the dysfunction, after my mother had left, my father would tell us how she could be the sweetest, most caring person in one moment, but then she would turn and be the total opposite in the next. He would say, "When she was nice, she was *very* nice, but when she was mean, she was *very* mean."

My grandmother often told me how smart my mother was and what a gifted pianist she was.

Whenever I heard people recounting all of these nice things about my mother, I wished she had stayed. However, when I think about her struggles, I feel grateful that she left to get the break she needed.

My father would often make statements that gave me clues about how he felt about her and her leaving. I did not like or agree with most of what he said. Since I blamed him for her absence, it was hard for me to understand his fury. I felt he was just making excuses.

Here are the statements he would make and how I felt whenever he would say each of them:

"I had to knock some sense into her." Whenever he said this, I would feel sad and did not believe him. I felt like he was just offering a dumb justification for hurting my mother. Even at my young age, I felt there was no excuse for him to have ever put his hands on her in anger.

"Your mother left, she doesn't want you." Both my father and maternal grandmother sat me down and told me this. My initial response was, "Well, if she don't want me, I don't want her *needer*." Grandmother thought my reaction was cute. I always felt like it was horrible for them to tell me my mother did not want me. As I grew older and thought about the issue, a part of me believed she wanted me. I felt they were just telling me she did not because they resented her for leaving.

I often thought, "What mother doesn't want a sweet little girl like me?" I felt like she ought to love and want me. I felt like she was just unable to care for me. That one comment, "she doesn't want you" was a big precursor to my feelings of rejection and insecurity throughout my entire life. However, I have always felt grateful that she did not take me with her when she left.

Being only two years old, and the baby of my six siblings, I often imagined that she could have easily picked me up and taken me with her. Had she done that, I believe I would have ended up separated from her. That is what happened to all of the children she had after she left us. In that case, I would never have known any of my siblings.

"She never did anything for you all." As a little girl, I felt like it was my mother's mental illness that made her incapable of doing anything for us. I felt like my father did not understand that. I could feel his pain whenever he would say it, but unfortunately, she just was not able to help him care for us. In reality, *she* needed someone to take care of *her*.

"She did not want children, but didn't believe in birth control or abortion either. When she finally got some birth control pills, she would forget to take them." My mother had six children by the age of thirty and I believe this overwhelmed her. I have always understood her not wanting a lot of children, not believing in abortion, yet not believing in birth control. That was a lot of pressure for her to have to deal with. It seemed the full responsibility was on her as the woman.

When my father would talk about it, I felt he was not taking any of the responsibility and placing all the blame on her. I think my father may have been feeling a lot of guilt for continuing to get her pregnant. I guess back then, men could not do much when it came to birth control. It was the total responsibility of the woman. I believe my mother's mental illness made the situation even more difficult.

He mocked her voice as he reminisced about the way she used to say, "One of these days I'm going to go far, far away." Whenever my father altered his voice to mimic hers, I felt like he did not take her seriously and he should have. She obviously really felt that way because she actually *did* go far, far, away when she got the chance. However, he did not believe her at the time. I believe he thought those words were spoken out of her frustration.

He mimicked her as he recalled how she said, "I'm in love with Calvin" just before she ran away. Calvin was a patient in the mental hospital she was in at the time. People may have called my mother "crazy," but she had enough sense to leave an abusive relationship. So, when my father mimicked her about leaving with Calvin, I never blamed her for it. However, I would always wonder what Calvin's last name was. I wondered if she ever married him, if they stayed together after they had run away together, if they had any children together and if so, how many. So, hearing those words, "I'm in love with Calvin" brought all types of questions to my mind…questions I strived to answer in my quest to find my mother.

"She couldn't keep a job." My father often complained about how my mother got a job working for a dry cleaner and was terminated when she refused to do things according to her boss's instructions.

He would say, "You can't do things *your* way when you are working for someone else. You have to do what *they* want you to do."

Whenever he complained about my mother not being able to keep a job, I felt bad for him because I knew he needed her to work to help pay bills. I felt badly for her because I knew she was not capable of holding down a job due to her illness. Thinking about the challenge of this situation causes me to feel sad, realizing this was unfortunate for both of them. I truly feel bad for what my father had to go through.

"If you all ever want to look for her, I will take you." Whenever my father would say this, I thought, "Of course I want to find my mother," and I felt like he should have just taken us to find her instead of saying that to us. But, then he would follow with, **"But, she may not receive you all."** I did not understand why my mother would not receive us. However, I believed him when he said it and those words made me feel afraid to tell my father I wanted him to take me to find her. So, as much as I missed her, and as bad as I wanted to see her again, I never asked my father if we could go and try to find her.

The thought of my own mother not receiving me made me feel a very deep hurt and I could not even begin to comprehend it.

The thoughts my father shared after my mother left were his truth. They were his reality, the way he experienced it, but I just refused to accept his side of the story because I did not know how things went down for her. Not knowing her side was one of my many motivations for spending an immeasurable amount of time over the years trying to find her. Now walk with me as I take you through the actual timeline of my search.

Chapter 3
THE SEARCH

I began missing my mother from the moment I was told she left in 1969. As a little girl, I desired to find her, bring her home and take care of her. I knew she was ill, and I always felt that wherever she was, she probably needed someone to love her. Unfortunately, I was too small to do anything. Besides my father had said she may not receive us even if we were able to find her. So, even though I missed her, it was just not in my heart to actually search for her back then.

I had already felt rejected by her leaving, I did not want to risk feeling rejected all over again if I were to find her.

As I discussed in my foster care storybook, *A Gifted Child in Foster Care*, in 1974, my father left town for work, leaving my siblings and me in a house alone. He promised to send money. He even and asked my grandmother, my aunt, and a lady who was his girlfriend, to come to the house and check on us from time to time. Somehow, unpaid bills left us with no electricity, no gas, and no water. A bare refrigerator left us hungry. A broken lock on the front door left us feeling afraid. The Sheriff removed us from the home and we became wards of the state.

When I was seven years old and living in foster care, my caseworker took me to visit my grandmother. During the visit, she told me about a call she had received from a hospital in another state, asking her if she could take a set of twin boys that my mother had just given birth to and left in the hospital. The hospital also told my grandmother that my mother had left a baby girl in that same hospital three years earlier and that the baby girl was adopted.

My grandmother told the hospital that she was too old to care for the twins. Hearing this made my heart ache. I was disappointed in her as I felt like she did not care what happened to the twin boys. I did not tell her I was upset because I was afraid she would think I was being disrespectful towards her.

The thing is that I wanted to know those babies because they were my siblings.

Even at my young age, I felt that my grandmother should have at least had the twins brought to Kansas City, Missouri so that I could get to know them. Since I was currently living in a foster home, I thought she could have had them placed in a foster home in Kansas City so that they would be close to us. I never understood why she chose to leave the twins in another state. At that point, I knew that I might never have another chance to know my baby siblings.

After learning I had more siblings, I never heard anything else about my mother. However, deep down in my soul I wanted to find her, see her, know her, touch her, talk to her, and shower her with all my love. However, the reality of my circumstances did not allow it. My young age limited me from being able to search for my mother.

As I grew older, I began to realize I actually had the ability to search for her. Becoming a mother at eighteen years old is what urged me to move things along. Having my own baby girl caused me to marvel at how a mother could just walk away from her beautiful little daughter.

Feeling this way caused me to make my first attempt to search for my mother in 1985. I walked down the street to the local Social Security Administration office and asked if they could help me locate my mother.

A woman explained their letter-forwarding program to me. She could not give me any information, but instructed me to write and submit an unsealed letter to my mother and leave it. If she was able to find contact information for my mother in their database, she would forward my letter and it would be up to her to respond. The lady said she would be unable to tell me if contact information was found.

Finding Mother: A Journey of Loss and Love

I would never know whether or not the letter was sent unless my mother actually responded. I followed the instructions, but never received a response from my mother. I did not know of anything else I could do at that time.

Ten years later, I came across a book that would teach me how to be my own private investigator. It provided guidance about how to locate hard-to-find people. With that paperback in hand, I began searching again.

November 14, 1995

I requested the marriage license, including the application, from the State Department of Public Health, for my mother and father but no record was found. I had sent a seventeen-dollar check for payment of the fee, and my check was sent back to me with along with my application and request letter. I was not sure how their marriage license would help me locate my mother, but I hoped the application would provide some hint that would possibly bring me closer to finding her.

I later visited a couple of Genealogical Research Libraries. Someone had told me that I might be able to find copies of marriage, birth, death, church, and school records there. There was an option to search very old census data to find records for ancestors, where they lived, their names and ages, and who their neighbors were. Through my search of the old census records, I learned that many families did not have cars back then. Therefore, it was not as convenient for them to move far away the way we can today. As a result, many family members lived on the same block.

The Genealogical Research Libraries also had an option to search the Social Security Index by name or by putting in a social security number to determine if the owner of the number was still alive. I searched the Index to find my mother's social security number. I managed to find one for my father, uncle, grandfather and grandmother, but none for my mother, Geneva. Finding a social security number in the Index means the person is no longer living.

Finding Mother: A Journey of Loss and Love

As I could not locate my mother's, I concluded that she might still be alive, which heightened my hopes of finding her one day.

In addition to the Department of Public Health and the Social Security Index, during my search, I solicited information from resources such as: Bureau of Vital Records, Family History Center, and International Marriage Locator.

Online white pages were another helpful resource. I used it to search for addresses and phone numbers for my mother and the man who she ran away with, Calvin. I called one particular phone number for a Calvin with a Missouri address.

I chose to contact this particular listing because my mother and Calvin had run away from a mental institution in Missouri. So, I supposed Calvin may have possibly moved back to the state. When we spoke, he was very cooperative and told me he did not know Geneva and that he had no family in the area that we suspected my mother ran away to. After our conversation, I was convinced he was not the Calvin I was looking for. The main reason was because his voice sounded Caucasian and I believed the man my mother ran away with was African American.

March 28, 1996

I contacted an online people locator service, and they sent me a letter including information outlining how they are able to help people, like myself, find their lost loved ones. They gave two options. The first option was that they could provide me with the techniques to do the search myself. The results of my self-search would be sent to me in the mail. The second option was that they could actually perform the search for me. The latter would cost a whole lot more, however.

Their promise to me was that if I was unable to find my mother using the techniques they provided for option one, then, they would credit one hundred percent of my payment towards the cost of a full search that they would do for option two.

I did not end up using option two because I didn't have any reason to believe that their techniques would result in my finding

Finding Mother: A Journey of Loss and Love

anything more than what I had already found using the names I had for my mother.

That day, I searched for my mother's first and last name. I have a letter that they mailed to me informing me they were unable to find any information about my mother after searching their nationwide database. It was almost two years later before I invested in another online people locator service.

January 9, 1998

I miraculously obtained a social security number that was supposed to be for my mother. I also learned the current last name my mother was using. Both of these pieces of information were surprise findings. I had been searching for her under her maiden name and the last name she had acquired from marrying my father. My heart was filled with excitement. I could not wait to search for my mother using her social security number and new last name. I had often been told that I could find my mother easily if only I had her social security number.

Finally, I had the key to unlock the mystery of my mother's location!

When I searched, nothing came up under that social security number or the new last name. I proceeded to search another online people locator service and contacted some people who I felt could possibly know my mother or in some way be related to her. Some shared her last name and some did not.

When that was not productive, I did a name search in an online phone directory. I also used it to conduct an online search for addresses and phone numbers for Geneva using the current last name I had just found out.

My father had already told me my mother ran away with a man named Calvin. Now that I had her current last name, I presumed that the man named Calvin might have had that same last name. The online phone directory had no listing for a Geneva with that last name and one listing for a Calvin. But, it was not the Calvin I was looking for.

Finding Mother: A Journey of Loss and Love

My excitement about finding my mother with this new information was dwindling.

January 27, 1998

I searched again. This time, I ignored their last names because a private investigator had told me that a woman who is lost may have changed her last name due to marriage and so it could be harder to find her.

I sent a letter to four women named Geneva who shared her middle initial and date of birth. I informed the women that I had found their information through an online people search. The letter included my age and the names of my brothers and sisters.

I wrote, "I am searching for my mother who left my siblings and me when I was two years old[…]Please call me when you receive this letter to let me know if you are, or even if you are *not*, the Geneva that I am looking for." I invited them to call me collect, meaning I would pay for the long-distance phone call. Since this was in 1998, landline phones were still widely used and cellular phones had not become as popular as they are today.

I continued, "Or you can write me back using the self-addressed, stamped envelope that I have enclosed." I ended my letter by assuring them that my letter was for real and that this was a sincere search for my mother.

Well, all four of the women took my inquiry seriously because they each wrote me back to let me know they were not the Geneva I was looking for. One of them even followed up with a phone call to me! I felt happy to receive the responses, but, sad because my mother remained lost.

With declining enthusiasm, one day I sat down in a chair at my dining room table. I wrote a very long letter for my mother, beginning with, "Dear Geneva, my name is Grace, the youngest of the six children you left in Kansas City, Missouri back in 1969. Thoughts of you have lingered over the years and it is my dream to know where you are and how you are doing."

Finding Mother: A Journey of Loss and Love

In my letter, I recalled how my father use to hit her and how, in my heart, he was to blame for her leaving. "He did his best to keep us together after you left," I penned.

"My deepest desire is to hear from you. I am not looking for a 'mother,' but would like to be there for you if you need anything." I shared with her the feelings of rejection I had experienced while growing up, due to her not being in my life. But I also told her that I have since triumphed over those feelings and that my life was good now.

After writing a few memories I had about her, I ended the letter by saying, "All my life, I have yearned to see you again, and I refuse to abandon hope that I will find you one day."

I poured my thoughts into this letter…

but I never sent it.

Chapter 4
THE SEARCH CONTINUES

January 10, 1998

I sent an inquiry letter to the Superior Court, Records Information Center, requesting any public information they could offer about my mother. I submitted her name, including her maiden and her newly discovered last name. I also provided her date and place of birth, her mother's and father's name. I gave the city and state where she was last known to be living, along with the information about the three children I heard she had.

I let them know I was Geneva's daughter whom she had left in Kansas City when I was two years old and that I was searching for her.

I concluded my letter by specifically asking for any birth, marriage, divorce, and death records that were public record. In response to my letter, they sent me a brochure about "How to Obtain a Copy of a Superior Court Document," which let me know the various documents that were available, the costs, and an official request form for me to fill out and send back.

Two days later, I returned to one of the online people locator services to look for the name Geneva, since I had no luck with the social security number. None of the women named Geneva, with her current last name, shared my mother's date of birth. Therefore, they sent me a list of fourteen women named Geneva who did not share her last name, but who shared her date of birth. They indicated that if my mother had a last name change then one of the women named Geneva listed on the report could be her.

This search did not include phone numbers, and since none of them shared my mother's middle initial, I did not bother to reach out to any of them since I had already written letters to four women named Geneva from a prior search list, who actually shared her middle initial.

Three days after that, I received my own birth records from the medical center I was born in. I had ordered them on January 2, 1998. The records showed the names of the doctor who had delivered me. They showed my birth weight and height, and the exact time I was born. They even showed my temperature, pulse, blood pressure, weight, how much milk I drank, and even the level of pee and poop in each diaper daily for the entire five days I was in the hospital.

My birth records also listed my first name as "Girl" for the first couple of days after I was born. By the fourth day, it listed my name as "Grace." I presume I was finally given a name after about two or three days of my birth. I also noticed the middle name "LaJoy" was present on the discharge paperwork.

I had always known that was my middle name. I just felt surprised to see that someone had given it to me at the last minute.

Because of my beautiful and unique first and middle name, throughout my search, I always imaged that if my mother ever heard my name, she would immediately know I was the baby daughter she left so many years ago.

I was released from the hospital in excellent health.

My birth records showed that my father took me home from the hospital. They also indicated that my mother was a patient in a "state hospital" at the time of my birth. The full details were unclear. The discharge paperwork, that was supposed to be signed by my mother, was signed by my father.

In addition to my father's signature, the discharge papers included my infant left and right footprints and my mother's right index fingerprint. My father's signature served as certification that he compared the Ident-A-Band, affixed on me, with the identifying information in my record. It also served as certification that he had examined me and determined that he was taking home the right child.

Finding Mother: A Journey of Loss and Love

After reviewing my birth records, it occurred to me that maybe my mother was unable to take me home because she was in a mental hospital.

I presumed that the "state hospital" referred to in my birth records was actually a "mental hospital." It also occurred to me this might be the same thing that happened to the three babies that she had left in the hospital back in the early 1970s.

I presumed that she did not necessarily "leave" those children in the hospital, but was unable to take them home due to being in a mental hospital at the time of their births, causing the babies to become automatic wards of the state.

I was lucky enough to have a father who was able to take me home from the hospital when my mother could not.

January 20, 1998

I learned that one of the digits in the social security number I had received for my mother was incorrect and then I was given the correct number. With the right social security number, I searched online again. I still did not locate my mother. But, this time, I found a 1997 record for a person named Kevin connected with her social security number. The record showed a middle initial, last name, mailing address, phone number and a birth year of 1975.

I called the phone number and learned it was a college dorm. No one by the name of Kevin was living there. I felt like I had hit yet another dead end.

I thought it was weird that I was not able to find any trace of my mother with her social security number.

I also thought it was strange for my mother's social security number to be connected with someone who was born in 1975, especially since she was born in the 1930s.

I wondered if Kevin could be my sibling.

I conducted additional research on his full name, but I was unable to find a matching name anywhere.

Now that I had what I believed to a be a good social security number for my mother, I sent a letter to a federal government

Finding Mother: A Journey of Loss and Love

agency's Office of Disclosure requesting to locate my mother as a missing person. I included my mother's name, date of birth, her parent's names, her place of birth, and her last known address. I do not remember if I ever received a response from the agency. Obviously, I did not locate her as a result.

January 21, 1998

The last online people locator service I used was never actually able to find any women named Geneva who shared her current last name *and* date of birth. So, I requested a report for a list of women named Geneva who shared her current last name, with *any* date of birth, and with phone numbers included. I received a list of four people with a letter stating that with the number listings they found, there was a high probability that I will locate my mother. I called all four but, to my dismay, none of them turned out to be the Geneva I was looking for.

By this time, I had used the online people locator service to conduct several "Geneva" searches using all the last names I had for her; I even searched with no last name. I used it to search for Calvin and for my mother's social security number, all with no success.

Since I was unable to find my mother using her social security number, it increased my suspicion that she was locked away in a mental hospital. I had always heard she was in and out of mental hospitals before she had left our family. She had run away from one of them with Calvin, never to return. After she left, I had heard she had abandoned at least three newborn babies in a hospital in another state. So, my thought had always been that she was in a mental hospital somewhere in a different state.

April 27, 1998

I searched online business pages. I called and wrote letters to several state and county departments of mental health service agencies, asking if they could tell me if my mother was currently, or if she had ever been, a patient in any of their facilities. Many of

Finding Mother: A Journey of Loss and Love

my phone calls resulted in either "she is not a patient here" or a referral to other possible mental health institutions in the area.

Within three weeks, I received a written response from two of the agencies. A State Department of Human Services informed me in writing that they have no record of my mother being a mental health patient. A County Department of Health and Human Services, informed me in writing that, after a meticulous search with a combination of all possible last names, they found that my mother had never been admitted in their psychiatric hospital. The letter also stated they were going to submit my inquiry to another institution so they may search for her, too. I noticed both response letters were from each institution's Medical Records Administrator.

May 4, 1998

I received a copy of my mother's birth certificate from State Department of Health. To my surprise, it was a "Delayed" birth certificate, listing my grandmother as my mother's "birth" mother and my grandmother's husband (who was actually my mother's blood great uncle) as her birth father.

I had always known that my grandmother adopted my mother when she was two years old. I also knew she changed my mother's name, her birthplace, and changed her birth month, retaining the correct year of birth.

As you may have figured out, my mother's adoptive mother was actually my mother's aunt through marriage. A bit perplexing, I know.

The birth certificate did not appear to be a normal adoption, which left me wondering just exactly how my grandmother got my mother. My grandmother would often tell me the story of how she adopted my mother:

She would recollect, "My husband, Joe, and I went out of town to visit his family. While there, we met his great niece, two-year old Ginny. She was living with her mother, Joe's mentally ill niece. She had given birth to seven children and had lost legal custody of them all except her youngest, Ginny. When I tried to give her advice about how to take care of Ginny, she became aggravated and told me to 'take her.' So, I did."

Grandmother took Ginny home with her and changed her name to Geneva. Knowing that story, I was surprised to see Grandmother listed as *birth mother* on Geneva's birth certificate.

The next day, I sent a request and a blank check, with a note "not to exceed twenty dollars," to the Clerk of Superior Court. I asked them to search for a possible divorce record for my mother, Geneva and my father, Jerome between the years of 1967 and 1975. I sent an identical request asking them to search for a possible marriage record for my mother, Geneva, and Calvin between the years of 1975 and 1998.

Within one week, I received a response for both stating no record was found. They both sent my blank check back to me since they did not find the record I requested.

July 8, 1998

In search for more answers, I wrote a letter to the Department of Health and Human Services, Vital Statistics requesting marriage records for Geneva and Calvin during the years of 1968 through 1975. I received a certified statement of no record on file. I also requested divorce records for Geneva and my father during those same years; just in case my mother had filed for a divorce after leaving Kansas City.

After all of those attempts, Mother was still missing. Fatigue overpowered me. I felt like all avenues had been exhausted. It seemed Geneva would never be found, so I took a break from searching and just enjoyed my life.

It was during that break that I published my first book of poetry, began conducting workshops for aspiring authors, and earned my Doctorate degree.

September 11, 2008

My brother gave me a copy of my father and mother's divorce order dated 1971. He had held it for years, but I had not known he had it.

Finding Mother: A Journey of Loss and Love

In the past, I had been searching in the state I heard my mother had moved to. Since she was the one who left, I was thinking she was the one who had filed. I had actually forgotten how my father filed on his own in Kansas City.

I was around five years old at the time of their divorce. I actually remember my father talking about his intentions and efforts to divorce my mother because she had abandoned us, and he did not know where to find her to get her signature for the divorce paperwork.

I also remember his relief the day the courts granted him the divorce and custody of us, his six children.

Because of what my father went through to ensure the court awarded him custody of us, I felt like my father truly wanted us. This gave me a sense of security, like no one would ever be able to take me away from my daddy.

Finding Mother: A Journey of Loss and Love

Chapter 5
STILL SEARCHING

At one point during my search for my mother, I wanted to try to find some of her biological family. Since my mother had been adopted and had her name, date of birth, and birthplace changed, I did not know any of her blood relatives.

It was like my grandmother had erased any trace of my mother's whereabouts even before she ever left our family.

So, not only was it difficult to find my mother, it also seemed impossible to locate members of her birth family. I searched old census records, looking for Joe, my mother's great uncle who raised her along with my grandmother.

He was the only blood relative whose name I knew so I thought I would find him, which would then lead me to other family members who were connected to him. However, due to Joe having such a common first and last name, there were tons of them listed in the census records. As a result, it was impossible to tell which one of them was the correct one.

So, I gave up my attempt to locate my mother's blood relatives, and placed focus back on actually finding *her*.

I walked into a private investigator's office and asked if he could help find my mother.

When he learned I had her social security number, he said he could definitely find her. However, I would have to pay the required fee in advance. I informed him that I had searched my mother's social security number a few times and had not been successful in finding her. So, I was reluctant to pay a fee to learn something that I already knew.

Understanding my hesitation, the private investigator agreed to search first and then if he found anything more than what I had already found, I would be required to pay for the additional information. He searched and, just as I suspected, he was only able to find the person named Kevin connected with my mother's social security number, and nothing more. He was puzzled because he truly expected that he would be able to uncover more information with that number.

Once again, a search was conducted that did not lead to finding my mother.

I had a similar experience with a second investigator.

A third investigator tried to locate my mother at no charge as a favor to a young woman who wanted to be a blessing to me. Sherry was hosting a women's empowerment event, and wanted to find my mother and reunite us during the affair. It was her belief that the attendees would feel uplifted by my story.

She asked me to give her all the information I had of my mother. I cautioned her about the challenges I had experienced in my search even though I had her social security number.

She still seemed to have faith that her private investigator could find my mother, so I gave her the information and hoped for the best.

Leading up to the event, I felt like even if they did find my mother, I could not imagine her agreeing to a reunion in front of strangers. I doubted the investigator's ability to pull off the reunion. Nevertheless, I felt grateful for Sherry having the heart to want to try it.

Days before the event, she gave me the news that her investigators had been unable to find my mother. Since I had not really allowed my hopes to rise up, I did not feel let down. I still attended the event and had a lot of fun. After the event, I gave searching a rest for a while.

March 24, 2009

I had just finished writing a new book and was preparing a national press release to promote the paperback. It occurred to me to use that same announcement as an opportunity to try to locate Mom. So, I coupled information about the book and my missing mother in one write-up.

Finding Mother: A Journey of Loss and Love

Geneva had been gone for forty years when I publicized that press release. She would have been around seventy-years old, so I still had some hope of possibly finding her alive. After the press release was made public, I met a very helpful woman who had access to non-public resources that could help locate my mother.

She offered to help, asked me for all the information I had, and conducted a very thorough search for my mother. She found an address that she believed was my mother's. I used an online map to locate the address. I also searched online for the property report and found a possible owner for the property. It was interesting to find a potential landlord, but it was not helpful to my search.

I was not convinced my mother lived at this address, but I sent a letter to her there just in case.

I wrote, "My name is Grace. I am the youngest of the six children you gave birth to before you left Kansas City, Missouri in 1969. You were married to my father, Jerome, who is no longer alive." I continued, "Your other children and I are all doing very well and we have longed to see you again. I have searched for you for many years, but have not been successful in finding you."

I included my phone number and address and asked her to contact me. I even included a self-addressed, stamped envelope so she would not have to pay for postage if she chose to write me back.

I concluded, "There is a lot more I wanted to say, but I want to give you the opportunity to respond to my letter."

I never received a response and this fueled my doubt about that being her address.

April 2, 2009

The helpful woman's search revealed the same Kevin who I had located during an online search nine years ago. But, there was something special about the record she found. It listed a different middle initial, last name, and date of birth for Kevin. The record date was January 1997. I presumed this was the same record that I found for him back in January of 1998, but with a corrected name and date of birth.

Finding Mother: A Journey of Loss and Love

I was thinking that Kevin could possibly be one of the children my mother had after leaving us, thus my half-brother.

I did additional research on the corrected name and found several family members for him. None of the phone calls led to any new information so I eventually gave up on that lead. However, I never stopped wondering why my mother's social security number was connected with Kevin.

The next day, I sent a note with pictures to my mother through the Social Security Administration's letter forwarding program. Since so many years had gone by, I thought I would try again. The rules were still the same. They would notify me if they did not find a Social Security Number for her. However, they would not be allowed to notify me if they found an address or were able to forward my inquiry.

One month after I left the letter, I received correspondence from the Social Security Administration office, which included the pictures I had enclosed.

They were not allowed to send pictures, but they did not return my note. This led me to believe that it had been sent. I never received a response, so I was not sure if my mother just never received it, or if she received it and chose not to respond. The latter was hard for me to accept. So, I just told myself she never received it because that was easier for me to comprehend.

September 30, 2009

I published my foster care story, and purposely included real names for my siblings and mother, with hopes someone would recognize the names and provide information that would lead to finding Geneva. It had been forty-one years since she had left.

December 16, 2009

A television show producer learned about my foster care story through an online search and offered to assist me in finding my mother in turn for me coming on the show for the reunion if her search was successful.

Finding Mother: A Journey of Loss and Love

When the producer learned I had my mother's social security number, she said she felt very confident that their investigators would be able to find her. I told her of the past challenges I had with searching her social security number, but she was hopeful that their show detectives would have more success.

The thought of the show finding my mother and me being able to give my siblings the good news caused me to become excited and accept her offer.

She provided me with a twelve-page application to fill out and return; requesting my name, children's names, occupation, and information about the person I was seeking.

That long list of questions included, *"How will finding your relative change your life?"* I answered, "It would satisfy my longing to see her, meet her, and to know how she is doing." And, *"If you saw her again, what is it you would like to say?"* My response was, "I love her. I have missed her. I do not blame her for leaving."

It inquired about my entertainment experience and medical history. I felt puzzled about why they wanted to know all of that. Nevertheless, I answered all of the questions.

The last request was for me to nominate someone else to be on the show. I responded, "It would be great if you could find my three half siblings, whom my mother gave birth to after she left. Also, my five siblings, who my mother left, would possibly want to come on the show if our mother is found."

Finally, the entire application was complete and submitted. Hopeful emotions ensued as I waited for a response.

A few weeks later, the producer called, apologizing that the show was unable to locate my mother.

In my heart, that outcome was somewhat expected based on my prior search experiences. Still, feelings of disappointment arose because I had been hoping that maybe *this* would be the moment that I would finally be able to reunite with my mother...but it was not.

By now, I had sent numerous inquiry letters, hired investigators, examined public records, and conducted online people searches. Victory was out of sight and hope was dim…

Chapter 6
LOSING HOPE, THEN FINDING A GLIMMER

There were times when I searched actively for my mother, like when I got a new idea or a possible lead. Then, there were times when I ceased to search. It was during those inactive times that I felt weak in my hope, like there was nothing more I could do. As if I was never going to find her.

It was during those times when I hated to mention my discouragement to people, because I knew they would attempt to help by giving me things I could try.

I used to run after every hint people told me to try but, when nothing ever worked, I became annoyed. I felt tired of people telling me "You should try this" and "You should try that" when I felt like I had tried *everything*.

Searching and not finding anything was disappointing, but the times in between my active searching were the most frustrating.

I used to enjoy watching talk show reunions. Those types of shows once brought me hope that I would one day be reunited with my mother. However, after writing to several of the shows for help and receiving no reply, I became saddened. I began to feel insignificant, like my story was not important enough to be chosen. I understood that those types of shows received many requests and they could not help everybody.

But, still I could not help feeling slighted and overlooked.

As time passed, I realized my mother was getting older and older; the chances of finding her alive were becoming slimmer and slimmer.

These shows that once gave me hope, now caused me to become disheartened.

Finding Mother: A Journey of Loss and Love

One day, I was watching a talk show. On this show, a twenty-two-year-old woman was granted a surprise reunion with her biological sisters and mother after over fifteen years. They were all thrilled to find each other, but I did not feel cheerful for them the way I once did when I would watch reunion shows.

My optimism was fading.

Instead of feeling hopeful, I was beginning to feel resentful. Instead of feeling happy for the families who were reunited, I was beginning to feel mad. Instead of feeling inspired by their good fortune, I was beginning to feel hateful and jealous.

Because of my increasingly raw feelings, I eventually stopped watching reunion shows altogether. I purposely avoided those types of shows because they revealed the harsh reality that my mother was missing and I may never find her. I decided that if I could not find my mother, then I would try once again to locate her family members and maybe even try to find my siblings that I learned she had given birth to after she left.

October 31, 2013

I submitted my DNA to two online sites and began contacting DNA relatives that I felt could be kin to my mother. I located two female cousins who I thought favored my mother, and two male cousins. One of the males was a possible first cousin and looked just like my brother, and the other was a possible second cousin and had my mother's facial features. I spoke with each of them to see if we could determine a connection of exactly how we were related. The closest I got was learning that my first cousin's father was possibly my mother's biological brother, and that his grandfather was likely my mother's father.

It was a good feeling to find cousins related to my mother in some way, but I was still feeling hopeless about finding my mother.

December 17, 2017

I received a phone call from a longtime friend whose mother left her when she was two as well. She told me about a television reunion show, which specialized in cases like hers and mine, in

Finding Mother: A Journey of Loss and Love

which the person seems impossible to locate. She said this show had reached out to her with the hopes of finding her long lost mother. In her excitement, she asked me if I was still looking for my mother.

I told her I had lost ALL hope and was not interested in even considering making any more efforts to find my mother. I told her I had done absolutely everything in my power to try to find that woman and had zero motivation to try anything else. However, I wished her much success in finding her mother.

Believing my mother was nowhere to be found, I continued searching for my siblings. While looking for them, I began thinking back about my friend's phone call. I realized her hope actually rubbed off on me enough to consider going online and watching the reunion show that she had received the phone call from. Even though reunion shows had made me feel unhappy in the past, I mustered up some courage and began watching some of the episodes.

While observing the excitement of people who found their long-lost family members, in particular their mother, I felt so very jealous of them.

I felt like their reactions of shock and happiness were fake. I just did not like those people because they had finally found their birth mothers, while my mother's whereabouts were still a mystery.

I just did not feel like finding my long-lost mother would ever become a reality the way theirs had.

As I continued watching episode after episode, I felt amazed while witnessing people finding loved ones who were over eighty years old, which was the age my mother would be.

A very slight glimmer of hope crept inside my heart all of a sudden.

I began to wonder if maybe it could be possible for me to find my mother. I found an application on the show's website, filled it out, called the show and intended to send it, but I never found the courage to actually do it. I was afraid of my hopes getting crushed once again.

Finding Mother: A Journey of Loss and Love

In the meantime, I continued searching for siblings. I even located an investigator to try to find my siblings. It was rather difficult, however, because I had no idea what my siblings' names were. Furthermore, I did not know anyone who could give me even a clue of what their names might have been.

February 2, 2018,

I called a caseworker at the Department of Children and Families, asking if they could confirm whether my siblings were adopted through their agency.

I spoke with Elsie, who asked me for my mother's name and any information I had about when my siblings were born and what their names might have been.

I gave her approximate birth years based on what my grandmother told me back in 1974. I did not know their first names, but I told her I believed their last names might be the same as the new last name I found for my mother. She told me she would research their databases and follow-up with me by email with the results of her search.

One week later, Elsie sent an email, advising me that I may be able to request a copy of my siblings' original birth certificates, not their adoptive birth certificates. About one hour after that, she sent the follow-up email that she had promised.

Her email stated she was not able to determine if my siblings were adopted through their agency based on the information I provided.

She told me that if I find out their exact names and dates of birth, to feel free to contact her and she would check the databases again with that information. At the end of her email, she provided some resources that she thought might help me in my search.

Among those resources were the Department of Health, a few online adoption databases and some online DNA testing and genealogical services.

I responded to her email thanking her for her help. I also provided her with the name and date of birth for Kevin, the young

Finding Mother: A Journey of Loss and Love

man who I had found connected to my mother's social security number, and asked if she could check her databases for him. I told her that I had always wondered if he could be one of the half-siblings my mother gave birth to after she left. I told her I had done a lot of research on him, but never found anything.

Eleven days later, Elsie responded to my email letting me know she was unable to find any matches for Kevin. She also told me that their databases were not set up to search social security numbers, so she was unable to search to see if they had a case for my mother.

She again wished me luck in my search and told me that if I get more information in the future she would be happy to check their databases again.

I thanked her again for her help and told her I would be sure to reach out to her if I got more information. Even though her efforts had been unsuccessful, I felt grateful that Elsie was so nice and helpful to me.

I continued to watch episodes of the reunion show, endlessly imagining how I would feel if I were to miraculously find my mother; all along believing it was impossible and sensing it was best to only focus on finding the children she had after she left.

In the meantime, my big sister Carla had been missing for several years and was nowhere to be found. I am referring to the big sister I grew up with and lived with. Carla had been clean from drug use for over five years, when she moved away from Kansas City. While living out of town, she reported that her life was going well. She was even providing counseling to other drug users.

The last time I saw her was when she had come to Kansas City for a visit. She looked beautiful, wearing a stylish red two-piece skirt suit, a shoulder-length wavy hairstyle, and evenly-applied makeup. We went to church together and ate dinner at a restaurant afterwards. She came to my house, where we talked and looked at pictures. Carla loved pictures!

Finding Mother: A Journey of Loss and Love

After she returned to her home state, we talked on the phone a few times until suddenly her phone service was disconnected. My siblings and I lost contact with her for about four years. Finally, I located her daughter, my niece, and *she* did not know where her mother was!

Apparently, Carla had come upon some very hard times and did not feel like she could ask anyone for help. She became homeless at one point and eventually went missing. She was a great sister who had always been very kind and loving towards me. I feel sorry for the adverse turn of events in her life and I often wish I could have done something to keep it from happening.

It has been well over ten years since she had been lost. Every once in a while, I would do searches to try to locate her.

Chapter 7

I Found My Mother!

March 2, 2018

On this day, I opened an account with an entirely different online people locator service in an attempt to find my oldest sister, Carla. I found some information about her, but was unable to locate her. I had five days of unlimited searches.

After I finished my search for my sister, I decided to perform one last search for my mother.

I did not really expect find her, but I felt somewhat hopeful that I might at least find some information about her. I definitely did not think I would find her alive. I searched and for the very first time in all of my years of searching, I received a hit for my mother's name, exact state, and date of birth! I even saw a current email address for her. I was thinking I had actually found current information for my mother and feeling like this could actually be the end of my very long journey.

However, I was scared to get happy too quickly.

In the past, I had been able to find numerous women with my mother's current first and last name, but none who shared both her state and date of birth. I had also been able to find those women named Geneva earlier who had the same date of birth as my mother, but with no matching last name or location.

I had written a letter to every one of those women named Geneva, on January 8, 1998, with no success, but this search was different.

After all these years, I felt hopeful in my heart that this might actually be her. I wanted to call my oldest brother, Jerome, and tell him the news right away, but it was just so hard to believe. I was afraid to become excited until I knew for sure. But, how would I find out for sure?

Finding Mother: A Journey of Loss and Love

As I examined the report closer, I noticed an eighty-something-year-old man, with a different last name, living at the same address. It appeared that my mother could be living with an older gentleman. When I searched for the address online, I found the official name of the residence, and it appeared under the category of Nursing Homes. I presumed that my mother was living in a nursing home and that the man in question was a resident in the same nursing home.

Further online research uncovered a phone number to the nursing home. When I called the number, the phone rang several times then gave a busy signal. I called the phone number from late morning until early afternoon and the same thing kept happening. I did some more online research to try to find a phone number to a location nearby, close to the nursing home address.

I called a nearby nursing facility and spoke with a woman who informed me that the address where my mother appeared to be living was actually a boarding home where numerous people resided.

She told me that the address in question was just one of many boarding homes in the area.

At that point, I called my brother and shared with him my suspicion that I think I may have found our mother, but that I was still trying to figure things out.

My brother asked me what name I had used to find her.

I told him I found her under the current last name she is using and told him the name. I told him I did not want to share all the information with him yet because I was still researching.

Little did I know he took the name I gave him and immediately researched for himself and found the exact same information that I had. Within minutes, he had done an online search for himself then called me back with the same nursing home conclusion that I had come to. He pretty much recounted what had happened to me: a phone that was never picked up.

Finding Mother: A Journey of Loss and Love

We both kept trying for hours to call the phone number with hopes someone would eventually answer. Finally, at around seven o'clock that evening, I called the phone number one last time.

This time, a woman actually answered the phone! Her name was April. I explained to April that my mother left my five siblings and me with our father when I was only two years old; almost fifty years ago. I told her that I did an online search and it appeared my mother might be living at this boarding home.

She asked what my mother's name was.

I told her the first, middle and last name and asked if there was an older woman with that name living there.

She said there was a Geneva who had my mother's last name, but she did not know her middle name.

I told her my mother's date of birth and asked if it matched the Geneva who lived there.

April confirmed that it was a match!

Still in disbelief, I went on to describe Geneva's skin color. She said my description sounded about right.

When she described Geneva's facial features, my hope increased that this could actually be my mother.

April said it sounded like we were talking about the same Geneva, but she said Geneva never said anything about having children.

"I had always wondered if she had children," April said. "She always acted evasive whenever the subject would come up." She continued, "This all makes sense now."

By this, I think April suspected Geneva's evasiveness may have been a sign of her deep-rooted pain of living so many years without her children, or maybe a show of embarrassment for having abandoned us.

Suddenly, April asked me a question that I was not expecting. "Would you like to talk to her?"

I responded, "She can talk!"

Finding Mother: A Journey of Loss and Love

You see, I always imagined my mother being immobile, lying in bed at some mental hospital, unable to talk due to being all drugged up. Therefore, when April offered to *go get her* so I could *talk to her* I felt stunned. That was not something I expected to hear at that moment.

April said, "Yes, she can talk," and called her to the phone.

Those few moments of waiting for Geneva to come to the phone felt so surreal. "Am I a really getting ready to hear the voice my own mother after all of these years?" I asked myself.

When Geneva came to the phone she said, "Hello."

Her older, scratchy voice did not sound at all the way I expected. I thought it would sound similar to mine, or my daughter's, or at least similar to one of my sisters'. A part of me really did not think this was the woman I was looking for.

"Hello, is this Geneva?" I said.

I felt my voice trembling, but I strived to maintain my composure.

She said, "Yes."

I told her I believe I may be one of the six children who she left in Kansas City almost fifty years ago. I was so nervous that I did not tell her what my name was. I was too busy trying reassure myself of her identity.

I proceeded to ask her some identifying questions.

She answered "yes" to them all in a very calm tone of voice.

Then she asked, "Who is this?"

I felt puzzled about why she asked who I was after she had already answered all of my questions. I felt like if she knew she had abandoned six children, she should have known I was one of them. In hindsight, maybe she needed me to calm down and tell her my name and explain exactly which one of her children I was.

I said, "If all of your responses to my questions are true, then I am your daughter."

She said, "You don't sound like my daughter."

I asked her to confirm her date of birth.

Finding Mother: A Journey of Loss and Love

She said, "I'm not answering any more questions because I don't know who you are." She took the phone away from her mouth to talk to April, who was standing beside her while she was talking to me. She said to April, "This doesn't sound like my daughter. This is not my daughter." Then she said to me, "I don't want to talk to you anymore."

April whispered to Geneva, "Ask her to come and see you so you can be sure."

Geneva said, "Come see me."

Those words made me feel very excited and hopeful.

I asked her, "If I came to see you, would you actually talk to me?"

She said, "Yes. Come on," as if she thought I was close by.

I explained to her that she was in a different state and I was in Missouri, so I could not just come right over. But, that I would come as soon as I possibly could. I told her it might be some days or maybe a week or two, but I would definitely be there. I also told her that when I arrive, I would be bringing some of her other children with me. I told her we had all missed her and wanted to see her.

She said, "Okay, come on."

I said, "okay" and asked her to put April back on the phone. I asked April if Geneva actually understood what she was saying to me; and if she was able to understand what I was saying to her.

April assured me that indeed she understood everything I said and that she communicates very well.

"When she has a problem, or if she needs something, she comes to the office and clearly expresses what is on her mind," April said.

I told April that Geneva had confirmed all of the information that I had asked her. I told April I was concerned because I actually asked the questions and Geneva simply replied, "yes" to my questions. She did not actually volunteer any of those facts.

April assured me that Geneva fully understood what she was saying, "yes" to. She told me Geneva was nice and quiet and that she does not bother anybody, she is compliant with taking her medications, she gets up every morning, takes a shower and puts on clean clothes.

"She never has a bad odor like a lot of the other patients who live here," April said. "Her only vice is that she *loves* to smoke! She is in good overall health, except she walks slowly, with a limp, because there is something wrong with her hip."

She also confirmed that my mother has a mental illness.

April continued, "She is fine as long as she takes her medicine. If she were *my* mother, I would bring her to live in my home with me."

She told me how excited she was that I had found my mother, and about the reunion that was soon to take place. She explained that the people who live there do not have families or people who call and come visit them. She told me Geneva had been living there for fifteen years and nobody had ever called or come to visit her.

She continued, "So when you said you were her daughter, I hurried up and brought her to the phone. We totally support families who are searching for their long-lost loved ones."

April expressed to me that she was very excited about this reunion and that she could not wait. She asked me to be sure to let her know when we were coming so she could make certain she was present for the reunion. She said she did not want to miss this moment. However, she also wanted to be there to support Geneva since this would be a very emotional moment for her.

"I don't want you to think you are coming to some nice place. When you and your brothers see where she is living, you will want to take her up out of here immediately," She said.

She also advised that we probably should not let Geneva know the exact date we were coming because there was a chance

Finding Mother: A Journey of Loss and Love

she could purposely "run" to avoid meeting us after all of these years.

When I hung up the phone after speaking to my mother and April, I felt a sense of disbelief.

I called my brother, Jerome, and told him I finally got an answer at the phone number that he and I had been dialing all day long. I told him that I actually spoke to our mother! I told him everything she and I had discussed.

So, when my brother got off the phone with me, he tried calling the phone number one more time and he managed to speak to our mother, too!

He called me back immediately after their talk. His conversation with her was similar to mine. He asked her a few questions about herself to confirm that she was really our mother, and she answered them until finally she insisted that she would not answer any more questions about herself because she did not know who he was.

She ended their conversation by telling him to come see her.

After comparing the details of our conversations, my brother and I felt that we had indeed just found our mother. So, we told our other two brothers and we all became excited about taking a trip to finally meet our long-lost mother for the very first time in almost fifty years!

All of those years of searching finally came to fruition.

The years I almost gave up were overshadowed by the fact I had found my mother!

To learn what happens during the trip, after we arrived, and how our mother reacted when she met us, please turn the page and begin reading *Reuniting with Mother: A Story of Tenacity*.

Finding Mother: A Journey of Loss and Love

Book Two

Reuniting with Mother: A Story of Tenacity

During the time period of this story, the author was very aware that her mother had a mental illness. However, she did not know her actual diagnosis.

DEDICATION

To my three brothers, "Jerome," "Grayson," and "Terrance." It was awesome to be able to travel with you all to reunite with our mother. I feel grateful that we were together during that emotional experience.

To my two sisters, "Carla" and "Danisha." I wish the two of you could have been present at the reunion.

To my two children, Aric and Arica. Thank you so much for your support throughout the years and especially during my reunion with Geneva

To my mother, "Geneva," who I finally saw again after forty-nine years.

FOREWORD

Secondary students would absolutely benefit from this book.

One skill that I would like to see increased in our students, is conflict resolution. As educators, we must do our part to ensure that we are equipping our students with the proper skills to become competent and productive members of society. Conflict is a guarantee as our youth transition from students to adulthood, so it is vital for them to learn how to handle the situations that cause it and advocate for themselves, while remaining respectful and understanding. This book provides a great example of that.

~Jacob Kelow, M.S.Ed.
Secondary School Counselor
Kansas City Public Schools

PREFACE

After I had located my mother, my three brothers and I traveled to meet her for the first time in forty-nine years. While we were out of town, we made three visits to the boarding home where she lives. In *Reuniting with Mother*, I uncover what happened during each of the visits and reveal my account of the events.

To help you follow the story a little better, my father and mother had six children together. Here are the fictitious names for each of them as shared in the story: Jerome, Grayson, Carla, Terrance, Danisha and myself, Grace. The story will reveal why my two sisters were not with us during the reunion.

INTRODUCTION

After I found my mother, there was only one thing I desired: to reunite with her as soon as I could! Thoughts of seeing her after all of these years were overwhelming. To look her in the face and tell her how much I had longed to meet her again was my heart's sincere desire.

I was experiencing bouts of disbelief. Is this moment for real? Was that actually my own mother that I spoke with on the phone? I found solace in knowing my brother, Jerome had spoken to her, too, and he believed it to be her.

Chapter 1
AFTER FINDING MOTHER

As soon as Jerome and I felt comfortable that we had indeed found our missing mother, we decided to share our news with our other siblings. Jerome informed Grayson of the news while I told Terrance.

That night when I told my two children that I had finally found my mother, their grandmother, I could barely keep my emotions at bay.

My daughter could not believe I had found her after all of those years. She was extremely happy for me, but she had gotten used to not having a maternal grandmother so she did not feel the need to go and unite with her immediately.

My son was shocked, too. "That is amazing!" he said. He was very joyful for me but, like my daughter, he did not feel a connection with his newly found grandmother. So, he did not have a deep interest in rushing to meet her either.

I understood where they both stood. However, it was eye-opening to witness my children not sharing the same endearment towards my mother as I felt.

I was ready to go to her right away.

I had waited forty-nine years and did not want to wait one minute longer.

I considered renting a car and driving out of town immediately that very night or early the next morning. Basically, as fast as humanly possible.

When I informed my daughter, son and brother, Terrance, of my intent to travel right away, they each warned me of a winter storm warning in the area where my mother lives, and encouraged me not to drive.

I felt frustrated. I had finally found my mother, now here was yet another obstacle to overcome.

Finding Mother: A Journey of Loss and Love

They suggested I should take a plane instead since it would get me there quicker anyway. Driving would be a seventeen plus hour drive, while the plane would be only a three-hour trip. I took heed of their warnings and decided to wait until after the foul weather had passed. During my wait, I made up my mind that I was going to travel there by plane.

There was only one problem: purchasing a plane ticket at such short notice would be expensive.

Excited about me finally finding my mother, my daughter paid all my expenses to reunite with her, which included my plane ticket. "Let me know if you need anything else" she told me.

Due to the winter storm warning, I was left in limbo wondering what day would be the best day to travel. Realizing I could not leave immediately and that I would be traveling by plane, my brothers and I discussed the possibility of traveling together.

The big question for me was, "When can we leave?"

I only got a couple hours of sleep that night, worrying about how soon I would be able to get out of town to see my mother.

The next morning, I received a group text from Jerome suggesting we leave that upcoming Thursday, March 8th and return on Sunday, March 11th. His text put me at ease. It put us all on the same page. I was able to calm down knowing we would all be together during this very emotional experience.

I texted him back informing him that, "this sounds good to me." We discussed our plans by text and phone until we finally agreed on the details of our flight, hotel, and rental car.

From the afternoon of March 3rd until the morning of March 8th, I eagerly awaited the moment that my brothers and I would finally board the plane.

Ironically, on March 5th, I received an email from the private investigator that I had contacted just days before I had found my mother. I had told him of my failed attempts to find my mother and asked if maybe he could help me find my siblings. Well, in his email, he asked me if I would still like for him to look into finding my siblings, and possibly even my mother. He said he was willing to "put some time into the matter, but can't guarantee anything." He said he believed he had some solid leads and all I had to do was to give him a few hundred dollars to get started.

Feeling as if he was trying to take advantage of me, I was happy to respond to his email, letting him know I had already found my mother and that I was preparing to go out of town to reunite with her.

The night before the trip, I packed everything I needed. I also packed some pictures. I found it difficult to choose among my photos and I wondered how many would be enough. At first, I thought I would only take some pictures of my two children and myself. Then I decided to throw in a few more of my father, brothers and sisters and their children. I did not think I would need all of those. I just felt it would be better to have too many than not enough.

After I was all packed, I took a shower and put on the outfit I was going to wear. I woke up at two o'clock the next morning and put my suitcase in my car. By three o'clock, I was driving to my brother Terrance's house to ride with him to the airport. When I arrived at his house, he took my suitcase out of my car and put it in his truck. We drove to pick up our other brother, Grayson so we could all ride to the airport together. We pulled up at Grayson's home and Terrance got out of the truck and helped him put his suitcases in the back.

Finally, we were on our way to the airport.

My third brother, Jerome, was traveling from another state. He was going to meet us there. After takeoff, our plane flew from Kansas City to a connecting flight.

While we were in the air, I remembered how my father would say, "If you all ever want to look for her, I will take you. But, she may not receive you all."

Therefore, I had no idea what to expect or if she would even talk to us. However, there was one thing I knew: that I was extremely excited.

Finding Mother: A Journey of Loss and Love

I felt that however things went down, I would be satisfied just for having found her.

We were sitting on the plane after landing at the connecting airport. I was in between Terrance and Grayson. We were feeling restless, eager, and somewhat fearful of what was to come when we finally reached our destination.

As we waited for permission to get off the plane, I pulled out my phone and began recording a video of myself talking about how I was feeling at that moment.

I stated, "I am very tired and anxious, yet nervous."

I was feeling zealous as I awaited the moment that our travel would finally come to an end, resulting with us being in the presence of our dear mother.

"Are you all okay with being on camera?" I asked my brothers.

"Yes, that is fine," Terrance replied.

Grayson felt a little shy as he laughed, "Oh, go ahead, I don't mind."

"So, how are you guys feeling right now?" I asked.

Terrance was sitting on my left, so I aimed my camera phone towards his face first.

Looking into the camera, he said, "I'm ready to be finished flying."

Then I turned to my right.

Grayson stated, "I'm tired and sleepy, but I am ready to see my mom!"

I felt anxious to get off the plane and board the next plane.

When we got off the plane for our layover, we were all hungry, so we bought some food, sat in the airport food court and ate before we finally boarded the connected flight, which would land us in the same location as our mother!

We sat patiently on the plane as it rolled up the runway, into the air, and above the clouds. To keep from feeling bored or anxious, I slept and worked some puzzles until finally our plane was preparing to land. My enthusiasm was immeasurable and I could not wait. Gazing out of the window, I saw one of the large wings of the plane and the clouds below us. I watched as the plane began to maneuver down into the clouds, then out, and slowly down onto the runway.

I could hardly believe that we had actually arrived!

As I looked out of the airplane window, I could see remaining snow on the ground from the snowstorm I had heard about before we left Kansas City.

The plane stopped and finally we were able to get off the plane.

As we walked through the airport to go pick up our rental car, I said a short prayer hoping that everything would go well and that our mother would receive us. I uttered that prayer because I was afraid that my father's warning all those years back might come to be true. Had I really come that far only to have my mother refuse to see any of us? I dreaded the thought that my greatest fear may become a reality. After we had rented the car, we drove to our hotel where we met up with Jerome, who had purchased a separate rental car. As soon as we finished checking into our rooms and freshening up, we all got in one vehicle and drove to the address where our mother was.

We did not know what to expect. However, we were all very eager to be on our way to see our mother after forty-nine years!

Our drive to the place where our mother lived was long and traffic was heavy. Other drivers on the road did not provide right-of-way due to everyone trying to make ways for themselves in the hectic traffic. A drive that was supposed to be only twenty-minutes turned into an hour long. I thought we would *never* arrive.

We finally pulled up to the boarding home around four thirty in the afternoon. We parked our car in this very old, unkempt neighborhood.

Before going in, we sat in the car and contemplated about whether or not she would receive us. We thought maybe she would

Finding Mother: A Journey of Loss and Love

since Jerome and I had spoken with her on the phone. "Come see me," she had told us.

We finally got out of the car and began walking toward the large, old looking two-story boarding home. We paced carefully in the snow towards the front door.

Residents of the home were sitting and standing outside on the front porch and steps smoking cigarettes. Their coats and clothes were old and tattered. They all turned around and stared at us as we continued towards the house. While we were persisting in the direction of the smokers, I scanned their faces with hopes one of them was my mother. None of them appeared to be her.

As we walked in between them to get to the front door, one of the men asked if we had some spare change we could give him.

One of my brothers happily reached into his pocket and gave the man some change.

We entered the house, walked through a strong foul odor, over to the front office and asked for April. A woman named Ashley told us that April had gotten off work at four o'clock, so we had just missed her. April originally wanted to be there to make sure our mother, Geneva, would be comfortable with our visit. Since she was not there, Ashley took us back to Geneva's bedroom.

The hallway back to her room was dim, and not well lit.

The less than one-minute walk to her room felt more like five minutes.

Finally, I was getting ready to see the face of the woman who carried me in her stomach for nine months, for whom I had spent most of my life searching. I could not wait to see what she looked like.

Chapter 2
SEEING MOTHER AFTER 49 YEARS

We entered the room where Geneva sat on her bed wearing black jeans, a black skullcap and a grey fleece jacket under a black leather coat as if she was getting ready to go outdoors.

There were three beds in that room. I remembered April had told me she shared the bedroom with two other women, one of which was in the room. She was a heavy-set younger woman.

The tiny, older woman sitting on the bed, who was my mother, did not look the way I had always imagined she would.

I had a picture of her in my mind based off a young adult picture, in her late twenties, which I had kept since I was a little girl. The picture I had portrayed a woman who was well dressed, with styled hair, a round face with a smooth complexion, light colored skin, slightly slanted eyes, full lips, white teeth and a bright, beautiful smile.

The woman who I was looking at looked like the exact opposite and had the appearance of someone who lacked the necessities of life.

The cap she was wearing covered the frizzy grey hair that was sticking out on each side. Her face was oval-shaped, with a weary look in her eyes and only a few teeth left.

Seeing what she looked like brought back memories of how, as a young child, I desired to take care of her. I wanted to find her, bring her home and give her all of the love she deserved. As I stared at this estranged woman, I thought, "If she had been in my life, she would not look this way."

I had always thought I would recognize my mother if I ever saw her. I thought she would look just like me and that I would know immediately that she was my mother. Honestly, I do not know why, but I thought she would be taller.

This little woman was contrary to what I had expected.

Finding Mother: A Journey of Loss and Love

All of a sudden, I felt unsure if she was actually our mother. In that moment, I began to feel fearful that we might have traveled all of those miles just to reunite with a woman who was not our mother!

As soon as my siblings and I saw her sitting there, we immediately began to try to determine if this was our mother by asking her questions like, "What is your middle name?" and "What was your mother's first name?" and "Do you remember living in Kansas City, Missouri?"

She seemed afraid and overwhelmed by all of our questions. She looked up at my three big and tall brothers, then glared at me and said, "I don't know who you are. I'm not going to talk to anybody because I don't know you all."

We explained our belief that we were her children who she left in Kansas City almost fifty years ago. We told her we did not want anything from her, that we missed her and wanted to see her.

She looked at each of us again, and just when it appeared she might actually accept us as her children, she said, "You are not my people. Anybody can come in here and say they are my people."

Just then, her roommate exclaimed, "Geneva, these *are* your people! They look *just like* you and they have pictures of you."

"What do you have to do with that?" Geneva asked her roommate.

Then she turned back to us and said, "You all are strangers. I don't talk to strangers about anything personal. I'm not giving out any information unless I know who I am talking to."

We asked her what it would take for her to know.

She just looked at us and did not answer.

I told her I brought my birth certificate.

She looked at me as if she might be interested in seeing my birth certificate. Then she said, "No, I don't want to see that."

Just then, I reached into a bag that I had carried in, pulled out a gift, and showed it to her. "Ms. Geneva, I brought you a brand new, soft throw blanket. I will just leave it here," I said, as I went to place it on the bed next to hers.

Despite looking tempted to accept it, she said, "No, I don't want that." Feeling saddened and let down, I put the gift back into my bag.

In our disappointment, my brother Jerome and I asked her, "Do you remember speaking with us over the phone? You told us to come see you." We assured her she did not owe us anything, that we were not looking for any apologies, that we loved her and just wanted to see her.

She said, "No, I don't trust that," and continued to stare back and forth at each one of us, as if she wanted to get a really good look at what we all looked like. After skimming each of our faces, she did not receive us, just as my father had cautioned so many years ago.

I must admit, although I believed my father back then, there was a part of me that felt he may have been saying that out of his anger towards her. However, in that moment, I was actually witnessing the truth for myself; and it was sadly disappointing.

I felt like this would probably be the last time I would ever see her, so I took a really good look at her.

Our pleading with her to accept us seemed useless.

Finally, in a moment of sadness, Terrance announced, "I'm done. It has been so long, who cares anyway?"

With that said, we all turned towards the door of the bedroom and walked out with our heads held down feeling rejected and heartbroken. All the money we had spent, the time on the plane, the excitement, hope and anticipation we had while traveling turned into great despair and disappointment within a matter of minutes.

I could not believe this was happening. I felt devastated as we made our way towards the front door.

Ashley followed us outside. She was very nice and kind to us. We all stood on the sidewalk in front of the boarding home. She listened to how we felt about our mother not accepting us and she tried to encourage us.

She reminded us that our mother had a mental illness and that she may just need time to accept us since it had been so long since she had seen us.

Ashley claimed that Geneva never talks to her and that she usually has a hard time getting her to take her medication, whereas April had given us a completely different account.

Like April, Ashley was helpful and caring towards us. She acted very concerned about us having a successful reunion with our mother.

I told Ashley that I really wish April had been there. I felt strongly that we would have had a better outcome if she had been.

Ashley apologized to us for April's absence.

Anyhow, I wanted to come back the next day because I at least wanted to see what would happen if April was there.

She told us April would be there at eight o'clock the next morning and we were welcome to come back.

After finally walking away from the boarding home, we sat in the rental car with an "I give up" and "forget this!" attitude. Then, we all spent a few minutes talking about what we had just experienced.

I noticed my brother Terrance looked more like our mother than I had ever realized. Growing up, people always said my brother Grayson and I looked more like our mother than the rest of my siblings. However, I did not see Grayson nor myself in my mother's face at all. It was amazing to see what my mother looked like and which of my siblings looked like her.

After the comparisons, the sad fact remained we had just been rejected by our mother once again.

After some consideration, I said, "We should come back tomorrow, when April is here. Perhaps April can be of help to us."

After talking about it for a few minutes, we all agreed to return the next day and try once again to woo our mother into accepting us. We concluded that we had not traveled all of those miles just to give up now.

We drove back to our hotel and did our best to relax our minds. Grayson and Terrance went out to eat dinner together, while Jerome and I opted for a quiet dinner at the hotel.

At some point after we made our decision to return the following day, a very strong feeling of rejection came over me and I just wanted to leave and go back home to Kansas City as soon as I could. A distraught feeling caused me to actually forgot we had agreed to go back to try again the next day. My high hopes had somehow vanished and I shared my feelings with Jerome during dinner.

I cannot figure out why I suddenly gave up after being so adamant about us going back the next day. I just know that during our drive from the boarding home to the hotel, I replayed this one thing in my mind: The way Geneva looked each of us in the face and rejected us without any remorse. I absolutely did not like the woman who we had just encountered, and I did not want her as my mother.

After dinner, I retreated to my hotel room then called to tell my daughter and cousin how the reunion visit had gone.

Afterwards, I recorded a video of myself talking about how I felt. I had been recording my excitement about the trip ever since we were leaving Kansas City. I initially hoped to create an inspirational documentary of what I hoped would be a wonderful heartfelt meeting with our mother.

When things turned out to be disappointing, I thought, "I'm not recording my feelings about this." However, I felt like, "It is what it is." Therefore, even though things had not gone as calculated, I hesitantly recorded my negative reaction to a reunion-gone-wrong.

I talked about the heartbreaking situation we had just experienced; and how April had stated if Geneva were *her* mother, they would live together in the same home.

Finding Mother: A Journey of Loss and Love

The woman I saw did not look like the woman April had described.

I expressed how we were standing there, in front of our mother, listening to her as she told us we were not her people; how devastating that was for me; and how I felt worse for my brothers because I could see they were hurting and I could do nothing to help them.

While venting, I wondered what was worse, not knowing where my mother was, or knowing where she is and knowing that she did not accept me.

After recording my misery, I lay there feeling heartbroken, trying to see a positive side to having found her. I no longer had to search for her, speculate about where she could be, or wonder why I do not have a mother.

Witnessing her living in a state of poverty and suffering from a mental illness helped me to understand why she left us.

Nevertheless, it still hurt deeply.

I had always blamed my father for her leaving, but after this failed reunion, I was placing all the blame on her. This experience had left me feeling rejected because I had finally come face-to-face with my mother only to have her deny me.

In my pain, I thought back about our final few moments at the boarding home. Although I did not think I looked anything like Geneva, I noticed one similarity. She kept biting her lips. *I* bite *my* lips! I have always known I copied the habit from someone but could not, for the life of me remember from whom I had copied it. Observing Geneva, it was clear I had copied it from her before she left us back when I was two.

That night, I spent hours on the phone with the airline and rental car company trying to find a way to leave and head back to Kansas City. A smooth exit was not possible, so I finally put my head on my pillow to rest for three hours before it was time to wake up again the next morning.

Finding Mother: A Journey of Loss and Love

When morning came, my brothers and I had breakfast together in the hotel dining room.

While eating, Grayson asked me about my desire to return home. "I thought we had all agreed to go back to see Mother today."

That moment felt like a wakeup call urging me to remember our agreement. I told him I was in so much emotional pain after our first visit that I had actually forgotten our decision. "We should definitely go back and try again," I told him.

After breakfast, Jerome spoke with his mother-in-law on the phone about the results of our failed reunion. In all her wisdom, she encouraged us to go back one more time but not ask Geneva for anything, not even for her to accept us. Just give her a nice greeting card, our phone numbers, tell her we love her and let her know she could call us whenever she was ready.

I liked that idea and felt grateful for her advice.

And that's exactly what we did. Jerome made a list of all of our phone numbers for us to leave with our mother. He and I used the hotel printers to make some copies of the pictures we had brought along so that we could leave them with her. Grayson purchased a beautiful greeting card to give her and included some pictures of himself and his family in the envelope.

Little by little, our hope was rekindled and we were emotionally ready to go back and give it another try.

I felt happy that I was not alone in this venture.

We knew that our mother was away from the boarding home at the mental health treatment center, also called "the Center," where they provided games, group counseling, and mental health services, every weekday from early in the morning until late in the afternoon.

We pulled up to the boarding home about one hour before she was expected to return, with the hopes that we would finally have the chance to speak to April.

My brothers had noticed during our first visit, that our mother almost gave in to me a couple of times and that she seemed intimidated by them. They announced that I should go in alone this time, get her to open up, and invite them to come in once she was comfortable with my presence.

Chapter 3
WILL MOTHER ACCEPT US?

There was still some uncertainty in our minds about whether this woman was really our mother. After all, what if she honestly did not know who we were. I walked into the home all by myself, strolled into a room where two women were sitting and asked if one of them was April. They said, "April went out for lunch about three hours ago and has not returned."

I told them I was there to see Geneva. Before I could tell them who I was, they both exclaimed, "You look just like Geneva!" I told them I was her daughter, and that my brothers and I had found her after forty-nine years. Furthermore, that we had traveled all the way from Kansas City to reunite with her. I explained we came here last night and she refused to talk to us, or to accept us as her children.

The women looked at me with compassion in their eyes. They told me Geneva had not come back from the center, but she would be back in about one hour. They introduced themselves.

Miss Adams was the housekeeper. She told me I was beautiful and that I had hair just like Geneva's, which made me feel proud. She said Geneva was nice, quiet, did not bother anyone and takes care of herself. "She talks to me every evening," Miss Adams said proudly.

The other woman, Miss Davis assured me Geneva would talk to me. "She is just older. She doesn't know. Don't worry, she'll talk to you." She told me Geneva comes to her whenever she wants cigarettes and that she loves to smoke.

Miss Adams took me to see Geneva's bedroom. She had a smile and a proud look on her face as she told me how she made up the bed and how she cleans my mother's room every day.

Finding Mother: A Journey of Loss and Love

When I was in her bedroom the night before, trying to reunite with her, the mood was intense. So, I had only noticed the three beds. However, during this showing, more details stood out.

The walls had a light color paint and there was a large piece of framed artwork hanging on the wall next to her bed. There was a four-drawer dresser, two nightstands, and one closet, which Geneva shared with her roommates. The bed cover looked clean, the floor was shining and the room was free of clutter. After admiring the bedroom, we walked back to the room where we had come from.

Miss Davis suggested something that would definitely make my mother to talk to me. "If you bring her cigarettes, she will sit with you and talk."

Miss Adams added that it would also be nice for me to bring her some coffee, shampoo, and soap.

Miss Davis agreed that those things are okay but insisted that cigarettes were what she really wanted. As I was leaving, Miss Davis gave me an empty cigarette carton. "When you go into the store, just show them this," she said. "Ask for *cherry*, that's her favorite kind."

They both assured me I could purchase all of the items at the corner store just down the street. Just like everyone else we had encountered who worked for the boarding home, Miss Davis and Miss Adams were very patient, kind, caring, and showed concern for us having a successful reunion with our mother.

I said goodbye to them as I walked out of the front door and back to the car, where my brothers were eagerly awaiting my return. I told them what Miss Davis and Miss Adams had said about the cigarettes. Initially, they were skeptical until I explained further. Then, we all agreed to take a trip to the corner store and buy whatever was necessary to get her to talk to us.

We purchased an entire carton of her favorite brand of cigarettes, coffee, shampoo, lotion, deodorant and a bar of soap. Then we drove to a local restaurant to get a bite to eat. We went

Finding Mother: A Journey of Loss and Love

back to the boarding home and, again, I stepped out of our vehicle and proceeded to walk up to the front door.

Miss Davis was outside, walking away from the house towards me. She told me Geneva was not there yet. She pointed to a street corner and told me to look out for a big blue bus to pull up there very soon; and that Geneva would be walking off of it and going into the house.

We sat in the vehicle, intensely watching the corner and waiting for the bus. While waiting, Jerome gave me a list of all of our phone numbers he had made back at the hotel. He told me to be sure to give it to our mother. Grayson handed me the envelope, which included the greeting card and his family pictures. At this point, we were not sure how things would go when I went in there.

Would she accept me when I went in alone?

Would my brothers get an opportunity to go in?

Or would we go back home rejected and dejected?

Finally, the big blue bus pulled up and stopped at the corner, just as Miss Davis had said. The door flew open and out walked all the residents of the boarding home, one person at a time. Eventually, Geneva stepped down the stairs of the bus and limped across the street towards the boarding home. Just then, I remembered how April had told me there was something wrong with my mother's hip.

"That's her!" we exclaimed. I climbed out of the car and walked towards the house. She was wearing the same black jeans, black skullcap and grey fleece jacket under the black leather coat she had on the evening before; and she was carrying a plastic grocery bag in her hand. Her limping prevented her from walking very fast so I caught up with her as she was walking up the stairs of the house.

I said, "Geneva, hi." She looked at me and attempted to walk faster to get away from me. However, her hip pain would not allow her to walk any faster but she continued walking into the front door of the house. I wasn't to be dejected so I continued to walk behind

Finding Mother: A Journey of Loss and Love

her. "I brought you some things, some cigarettes and stuff. Can we sit down and talk?" I implored.

She stopped walking, turned around, looked at me, then looked at the bags I was carrying. Then she said, "No. I don't know you. I'm not going to talk about my life."

I said, "I just want to talk. I won't ask you about your life, okay? I'll just give you some stuff and you don't have to tell me anything that you don't want to share."

There happened to be a male resident, standing directly inside of the doorway, who heard my conversation with my mother. He looked down at the bag with a look on his face that said, "I don't know what her problem is, but if she does not want those cigarettes, I will take them." She kept walking and didn't say anything else, and I continued to follow her as she walked to the door of her bedroom.

I said, "We will just talk. I will have to respect the fact that you don't want to talk about your life, okay?"

She said, "No, I don't talk to anybody about my life."

I said, "I'll respect that. I understand."

Her bedroom door was locked because all room doors stay locked at all times. She turned to go ask one of the workers to let her in. As she walked into her bedroom, I walked in behind her.

She went over to sit on her bed in the exact same spot where she had rejected us the night before. At the same time, I was standing up pouring all the items my brothers and I had bought on to the bed next to hers. I noticed her eyes light up when she saw all of the cigarettes, but she still did not warm up to me at all at that point. She continued to keep her guard up as she looked at me with a very serious, untrusting look on her face. I continued to pour out the items.

I told her Miss Davis and Miss Adams had told me some of her favorite things.

The mention of Miss Davis and Miss Adams seemed to cause her to relax slightly.

Finding Mother: A Journey of Loss and Love

"They both said I look just like you," I told her.

She looked at my face as if to see if she could see a resemblance between her and myself.

"They said my hair was just like yours," I continued.

She glanced up at my hair as if to see if she thought I had hair like hers. It was at that moment that I began to feel like she was warming up to me just a bit.

"I am really happy to have finally found you," I told her. "It has been my dream to find you and take care of you."

I sat down on the bed where I had poured the stuff.

"Here is a list of our phone numbers that Jerome made for you. After we go back to Kansas City, you may call us if you need anything or if you just want to talk."

I showed her my birth certificate and pointed to her name to show her she was my mother. I showed her my copy of her own birth certificate and pointed to her name and her parents' names. She took it and studied it very carefully.

I asked her if she had her own copy.

She shook her head, "No."

I told her she could have that one, and asked for her permission to take a picture of it for me to keep since that was the only copy I had, and it was an original, certified copy.

She nodded her head, "Yes," and handed it back to me.

I whipped out my cell phone and snapped a picture of her birth certificate before handing it back to her.

"I brought some pictures of your children and family. Would you like to see them?" I asked.

She nodded her head, "Yes."

First, I gave her the greeting card and family pictures from Grayson. She opened the envelope, read the card then slowly, patiently and quietly looked at each picture.

Finally, she said something!

"Is this Grayson?" she said as she gazed at a picture.

I said, "No, that is Grayson's son."

Looking at a picture of Grayson's wife, she asked, "Is this you?"

"No that is Grayson's wife."

She continued to look at each and every one of Grayson's pictures very carefully, with much interest. It was at that point, I felt like she was beginning to warm up a bit more. I also knew she was not ready to allow my brothers to come in to meet her. So, I texted them to let them know she was looking at pictures.

When she finally finished looking at the pictures of Grayson and his family, I pulled out some more pictures. I showed her a picture I had of my father with my siblings and me when I was four years old. She held it in her hand and stared at it for a few moments.

She asked me if our father was still alive.

I told her he had passed away back in 1991.

She said, "Are you sure?"

I said, "Yes."

I went on to tell her some of the things that happened with our family after she left. I told her that my father ended up leaving us in a house alone to go work in Florida, and we ended up in foster care.

She said, "Oh yeah?"

The look on her face told me she was not happy to hear that, and I detected that she was experiencing some mixed feelings. The first was a feeling of surprise that my father actually left us. The second was a feeling of hurt for us ending up in foster care. The third was a feeling of disappointment with him for not being the dependable parent that he purported to be while she was still with us.

A moment later her countenance changed as if she was thinking she should not be judging him or saying anything bad about him to me. Yes, I detected all of that just in her facial expressions! I was surprised to see the looks of concern on her face since she had left us and never came back.

Finding Mother: A Journey of Loss and Love

It was hard for me to believe she actually cared about what happened to us after she left.

After that, I handed her some pictures of my children and myself. As she looked at them, I told her their names, ages, and what they did for a living. Then she handed the pictures back to me. I took them, but I handed a select few of them back to her to keep. She set them on top of the stack she had made while looking at the pictures of Grayson's family.

Then to my surprise she asked, "What about Terrance?"

Nobody had mentioned my brother, Terrance's name to her.

I felt amazed because this was the first sign of her showing that she actually knew who we were! This made me feel a little more confident that this woman was indeed my mother.

I pulled out some pictures that I had of Terrance and handed them to her. She looked at them with great interest. Noticing that I had not shown her any pictures of his family, she asked, "Does Terrance have any kids?"

I said, "No, he is married though, but I do not have any pictures of his wife."

I finished showing her all of the pictures I had of Terrance.

She looked up at me and said, "What about Danisha?"

Again, I felt amazed because no one had mentioned Danisha's name to her either! Nevertheless, I pulled out some pictures that I had of Danisha and her children. I showed her some pictures of Danisha as a little girl, as a teenager and as an adult. She seemed to take a special interest in one of the pictures; the one in which Danisha was nineteen years old and suited in her Army Uniform. She stared at it a lot longer than the rest, so I told her she could keep that one.

When she was finished looking at all of the pictures I had of Danisha, I showed her some pictures of Carla and her children. Then, I mentioned to her that we did not know where Carla was. She seemed genuinely concerned about Carla missing.

Finding Mother: A Journey of Loss and Love

She said, "That's weird that nobody knows where she is!"

When she said that, it gave me a bizarre feeling in my heart because she, herself, left her family and nobody knew where *she* was for almost fifty years! So, I did not understand why she thought it was weird that we did not know where Carla was. Once we were done talking about Carla and looking at pictures of her, my mother surprised me once again.

I was stunned when she asked, "What about Grace?" when I had been sitting there talking with her and showing her pictures for over an hour!

I said, "That's me. I'm Grace!"

She looked at my face as if to see what I looked like. It was at that point when I realized that maybe she honestly did not know who we were the evening before; and maybe she was not purposely denying us; and maybe she truly needed to be sure of who we were before talking to us.

When I really thought about it, I never did introduce myself or tell her who I was. I just walked up to her, said hello and followed her into the house and into her bedroom while telling her I had brought her some things and asking her if we could talk. I just assumed she knew exactly who I was. However, I learned a valuable lesson about reuniting with a long lost loved one after an entire five decades: you have to start from square one and be patient with the person.

Since I had already showed her pictures of my children and myself earlier, I took this moment to ask her if she thinks she will ever come visit us in Kansas City.

She blushed, turned her head to the side, laughed and said, "You're rushing me."

I laughed with her, then I apologized for rushing her. However, seeing her laugh made me realize how very important the pictures were in jogging my mother's memory and helping her to understand who we were. I was even wishing I had brought more.

Chapter 4
REUNITED

I felt like now that the pictures had helped her to recollect her memory, this would be a good time for my brothers to come in. I asked her if I could call my brothers in to talk with her.

She looked afraid and said, "No, not yet, I have some business I have to take care of before I can meet them."

I told her that they traveled a long way just to see her and they would feel sad if they had to go all the way back home and not be able to talk with her. I told her that if they do not get to meet with her while we were in town, there might not be another opportunity.

She said she was not ready.

Feeling afraid that she may never be ready. I asked her if I could ask them to come in one at a time; and assured her they would not ask her anything about her life.

She said, "No, not yet! I need to see them first."

I knew she was feeling nervous and confused so I told her that was why I wanted to bring them in, so that she could see them.

"So, may I call one of them in now?" I asked.

She looked at me with a nervous look on her face and did not say anything for about thirty seconds. Then, her face looked less afraid and she said, "Ok."

I became excited and asked her which one of her sons she wanted to reunite with first.

She said, "Wait, not yet! I'm not ready. I have to take care of my business."

At that point, I very gently reminded her that she said it would be okay if they came in one at a time.

She said, "Oh yeah, okay."

I asked her once again, which son she wanted to reunite with first.

She said, "Umm, Grayson."

Finding Mother: A Journey of Loss and Love

I told her I would go get him out of the car and I would be right back. Excited, I hurried out to car where my brothers were anxiously waiting, and told them she was ready to meet Grayson.

My announcement was met with confusion as they all seemed perplexed as to why she only wanted to meet Grayson. They asked me if she knew who we were now and if I was sure she was actually our mother.

In that moment, I had to focus on several things:

Getting Grayson in to the house to meet Geneva, before she changed her mind.

Explaining that she was more comfortable meeting them one at a time, and she chose Grayson as the first.

Calming their valid concern as to why I believe she is actually our mother.

Calming Jerome's disappointment about her choosing to meet Grayson first instead of him.

I quickly told Jerome I believe she asked for Grayson first because he sent in the card and pictures.

Grayson humbly asked, "For real? She specifically asked for me?" As he was opening the car door and stepping out onto the sidewalk.

I said, "Yes," and quickly explained to Jerome and Terrance that our mother was not comfortable with all of them coming in at once. I also rapidly told them that she specifically asked about Terrance and Danisha without me ever telling her their names. Then I rushed off to walk with Grayson.

We walked into the house together, went back to Geneva's bedroom and knocked on the door. She opened the door, we walked in, and she sat back down on her bed.

Smiling, Grayson walked over to our mother.

He gave her a hug and a kiss and she happily accepted. Grayson was careful not to ask her anything about her life. He talked to her about some fond memories he had held about her over the years. Specifically, he reminisced about a time when he was a little boy and he gave her some money because he knew she needed it. He told her that he and his family were doing well and that he was able to provide her with a better life if she so desired. He told her how much he loved and missed her.

The whole time, she looked at him and nodded her head in a "yes" motion, giving a smile every now and then.

Grayson ended his time with our mother by asking her if he could take a picture of her.

She said, "Yes."

Feeling jealous, I asked mother if I could have a picture with her.

She said, "Okay."

So, I sat beside her, she straightened up her cap and Grayson took the picture. Then Grayson took the picture that he wanted of her by herself. Mother seemed more comfortable and happily allowed us to take the pictures.

During the exciting picture-taking moment, after sitting next to her for the picture, it dawned on me how very small my mother's stature was. For a few moments, I wondered how my seven-foot tall father was able to bring himself to hit this tiny woman. She could not have been any taller than five feet two inches.

After Grayson enjoyed mother for a few more minutes, I asked mother which of her sons she wanted to see next.

She said, "Oh okay. I want to see Devon."

So, I asked Grayson if he would go out to the car and ask Jerome to come in. Jerome's middle name is Devon and my mother remembered him as Devon, but we now call him Jerome.

Grayson said his goodbyes to mother, then went outside to the car and sent Jerome in.

After a few minutes, Jerome knocked and I let him into the bedroom. He walked over to where our mother was sitting and gave her a big bear hug and a great big kiss and was very happy to see her.

She had a humungous smile on her face.

Like Grayson, Jerome was also respectful in not asking her any personal questions. Instead, he told her how much he had missed her. He reminisced about how he used to call her "mommy" when he was a little boy.

With a happy look on her face, she said, "All of my kids called me mommy."

Sitting on the bed next to hers, he recollected how she instilled in him a sense of spirituality and that he strives to be a good person today because of it. He recalled how she was a great cook and that she made the best homemade rolls and cookies.

She said she was not sure she agreed she was a good cook, but she certainly had a huge grin on her face the whole time he was talking about it.

Jerome told her he was a good cook, too.

She said, "Oh yeah?" and asked him what he could cook.

He told her he baked pies really well and that he cooks full holiday meals, complete with items like turkey, dressing, macaroni and cheese, greens, and corn bread. He even told her about the few times when he invited me over to his home to partake in the delicious home-cooked meals.

"You can ask Grace. She has been over for holiday dinners," he bragged.

At first, I teased him by saying, "He can't cook." Then, I immediately confessed I was just joking and that he was actually a great chef.

Jerome went on to tell our mother that he was doing well for himself. He showed her pictures of himself, his son, his house, his truck and his wife. He expressed how much he loved and cared for his wife. Then, he actually called his wife using the video chat feature on his phone to let our mother see her and talk with her.

"You are beautiful!" Jerome's wife said.

The compliment caused our mother to smile and even blush a little. It gave me a warm fuzzy feeling, too!

While they were chatting, one of Geneva's roommates

knocked on the bedroom door because she wanted to come in. I got off the bed I was sitting on, went to the door and opened it. She walked into the bedroom, went to the closet as if she was looking for something. While standing in front of the closet, she cleared her throat as a way of getting my attention. I looked over at her.

She whispered, "Do you have any change you could give me?"

Realizing I was actually sitting on her bed, I smiled and told her that since she was kind enough to allow me to sit on her bed then I would give her some change. I reached in my pocket, pulled out all of the change that I had and gave it to her.

She said, "Thank you," then left.

After the video chat, Jerome continued to reminisce. He recalled that our mother was a great piano player, that she enjoyed sewing and knitting, and how she loved to polish her fingernails! With a smile on his face he told her, "You used to *always* be sitting at the dining room table polishing your fingernails."

She smiled.

Absently I looked down at her hands, noticing chipped red nail polish on each finger. I guessed she still enjoyed polishing her fingernails.

Jerome's time with our mother ended in yet another photo session.

Just before leaving, he reminded our mother that she had his phone number and she was welcome to call him anytime. He told her that he was capable of providing for some of her needs, and she could feel free to ask. He talked with Mother for a few more moments, then, she was ready to meet Terrance.

Jerome lifted himself off the bed, said his goodbyes to mother, and went to the car to send in Terrance.

Within a few minutes, Terrance showed up at the door of mother's bedroom. I opened the door and in he walked. He began his reunion by giving her a big hug and kiss and telling her how much he had missed her. During his reunion, Terrance asked her if

Finding Mother: A Journey of Loss and Love

she liked living in the boarding home.

She hesitated, then, said it was okay but she did not like the residents stealing from her. She said she could not have anything of value there and that she used to have a television but it was stolen.

"Well, if you ever want to leave here and come live in Kansas City with us, just call me and I will make it happen," he told her.

"I will let you know," she said.

"I have a lot of business to take care of before I can consider moving."

Whereas, Grayson and Jerome did most of the talking during their reunions with our mother, she had become more comfortable and talked a lot during Terrance's reunion. At the beginning of her reunion with me, she did not want to talk about her personal life. However, by this time, she was sharing some very personal information about herself.

She volunteered the fact that she had ten children.

Terrance and I looked at each other with surprised expressions on our faces.

Then I asked her, "So you had *four* more children after you left?

She said, "Yes."

I told her I was aware of three of them who she left in the hospital, but not the fourth one. I told her about the call my grandmother had received from a hospital, asking if she would take her set of twins after she left them in the hospital. I told her that my grandmother was also informed about her little girl that she left in the same hospital three years before the twins. I asked her if she wanted me to try to find them.

She said, "Yes."

I asked her for the names of the hospitals they were born in and she gave them to me. I asked her for their names and dates of birth.

She told me their first names. She had difficulty recalling

Finding Mother: A Journey of Loss and Love

their dates of birth, but did her best to give me the correct dates. She said she used to have a list of all of her children's names and birthdates, but she had lost all of her belongings.

This was an amazing moment for me, because I had longed to find the siblings my mother had after she left. However, I had no idea of the children's names and I did not know anyone who could give me even a clue. Therefore, finding them had been close to impossible. Finally, here I was sitting in front of my own mother; and she was telling me the names she gave to each of them. I was able to acquire this long-awaited information directly from the person who named them! Something I never thought would happen in this lifetime!

I felt happy she was being so open after being so cautious at the beginning, but I did not want to hinder that moment. So, I treaded lightly as not to bombard her with all the other questions I had carried in my mind for so many years.

I put a little time, space, and careful consideration between each question. I did muster up the courage, however, to ask her if she ended up marrying the man named Calvin and if she and the additional four children shared his last name.

She said, "Yes," to both questions.

Then I asked her how long she and Calvin were together.

She said, "Two years."

It was very nice to learn details about what her life has been like since she left us five decades ago.

Terrance asked her how she was doing overall.

She said her hip hurts all the time, but otherwise she was doing okay.

I asked her if I could take a picture of her with Terrance.

She said, "Yes," but that she would have to smile with her mouth closed because she was very embarrassed about her teeth.

"I used to have some pretty teeth," she said.

"All of a sudden they just started falling out. I don't know what happened."

Finding Mother: A Journey of Loss and Love

She expressed how much she would like to have her teeth fixed.

I told her I knew she used to have pretty teeth because I saw them on the picture of her that I had kept all of those years. I snapped the picture of her and Terrance then she continued to talk openly with us.

As she went on talking, she recited Devon's date of birth. Terrance looked at me in amazement that she actually knew that information. She also recited Carla's middle name. I asked her if she remembered mine.

She said, "I didn't give you one."

I felt very surprised to learn that she did not give me my middle name. I told her it was LaJoy but it did not ring a bell with her. Just then, I remembered how my birth records showed "LaJoy" on the final days of my hospital stay, indicating someone added it at the last minute. So, if my mother did not give me that name, then who did I wondered.

While she and Terrance continued to talk, I veered away in my thoughts, thinking that my grandmother must have given me my middle name. I was silently remembering how she used to correct me whenever I stated it incorrectly. I used to think the correct way to say it was "Joy". However, my grandmother would correct me and say, "Your middle name is LaJoy with a 'La' at the beginning." So, then I began to call myself Grace "LaJoyce."

Again, she would correct me and say, "Your middle name is LaJoy, with no 'ce' at the end." Reminiscing about her insisting I stated it correctly led me to presume that Grandmother was indeed the person who had given me that middle name.

Towards the end of her time with Terrance, our mother had mentioned several times that she needed to go eat her dinner. She was careful not to make us feel unwanted, but she just really wanted to go eat. Finally, we realized how badly she wanted to go eat, so we rapidly began to wrap up our visit. We asked her if she needed anything.

Finding Mother: A Journey of Loss and Love

She said, "Do you want to know what I really need? Money!" then she laughed.

We had already planned to give her money, so we both took some bills out of our pockets and gave them to her. We were concerned about giving her cash due to the living environment she was in, because she lived with people who she said steal from her and who had begged us for money. Out of my concern, I asked her if she knew how to protect her money.

She said, "Yes." She kept it in her purse, which she wore strapped around her neck and across her chest at all times.

As we were walking towards the front door to leave, we saw the very large dinner rack. We also noticed there was only one plate of food on it so we guessed it was hers. In hindsight, we realized that if she had not come for dinner when she did, one of the other residents would have taken her plate and eaten her dinner.

After she had secured her dinner plate, I asked her what her favorite food was.

She said, "Fried chicken."

I asked her if she wanted us to bring her some the next day and have dinner with her.

She said, "Yes," with a smile on her face.

Terrance was in agreement with coming back the next day, too. As we were leaving out of the door, she reminded us with excitement in her voice, "Tomorrow at four o'clock, don't forget!"

We said, "Okay."

As we were leaving, we each hugged our mother and gave her a kiss on the jaw. In turn, she gave each of us a kiss on the jaw, too. We proceeded to walk out of the door and joined Jerome and Grayson in the car. We were talking about the very emotional reunion we had just had with our mother.

Terrance told Jerome, "Man, she knew your birthday!" And nobody had even told her!

He seemed amazed by that, which let me know that just like our mother truly needed to understand who we were, he truly needed to feel sure that she was our mother.

When we told Jerome and Grayson we had promised our mother that we would come back the next day with fried chicken, Grayson was okay with it. My thought was that since we were there to see her, then I expected we would spend as much time as we could with her. Jerome's thoughts were different.

"I will not be joining you all for dinner with Mother tomorrow," he announced.

I believe Jerome only needed the memory of reuniting with her and knowing that she was okay. I believe he found closure after she had accepted us. He wanted memories that he could share with his offspring, nieces and nephews, and he got that.

As he drove us all back to the hotel, I had time to do some silent thinking of my own. I initially felt like since Geneva was my mother, who carried me in her stomach for nine months, she should have accepted me immediately, no questions asked. What I did not think about was this: just like we bombarded her with questions at the beginning, because we wanted to be sure of who she was, she also needed the opportunity to be sure exactly who we were, especially since she had ten children, whom she had been separated from for decades.

She needed to be able to understand whether we were the first set of six children she left in Kansas City, or the second set of four children that she left after her departure from us.

I guess when a person has been living in denial about having children for so many years they do not just snap out of it in one moment.

I had to sit with her, talk softly to her, show her pictures, be kind and gentle and introduce my brothers slowly and carefully, one at a time, while eagerly hoping she would accept each of them before we traveled back to Kansas City.

I felt like we had just had a very productive day!

When we returned to the hotel, we ate dinner then retired to our rooms for a good night's sleep.

Chapter 5
OUR FINAL VISIT WITH MOTHER

That next morning, we ate breakfast together at the hotel restaurant. Then we went back to our respective rooms to rest up before going back to the boarding home for dinner with our mother that evening. While in our hotel rooms, Terrance and I got into an argument over the phone and I was feeling unloved. Therefore, when it was time to go have dinner with our mother, I was so upset that I announced I was not going. After a few minutes of drama, they ended up getting in Grayson's rental car and going without me.

The argument was not related to our mother but, at the time, it seemed huge. Looking back, it was mere sibling rivalry, which had soured my mood. However, at the time it appeared enormous enough to cause me to refuse to visit my mother, whom I had longed to know for forty-nine years.

After they pulled off, I began to think about how it was my idea to have dinner with her in the first place. I thought about how much I really wanted to have this moment with our mother. Most of all, I remembered how badly I wanted to ask her why she left and listen intently as she talked to me about it. So, I hopped into the rental vehicle that Terrance and I had purchased and drove myself to the boarding home.

They went to buy the chicken dinner first, so I arrived at the home before them. I texted to let them know I was there and waited for them to show up so we could all walk in together. I was still feeling sad, but I put on a happy face so that we could all enjoy this final visit with our mother. Finally, they arrived and we walked in at four o'clock, with a large chicken meal, as promised.

One of the workers met us at the door and asked, "May I help you?"

We told her we were there to have dinner with our mother, Geneva, so she gave us permission to proceed. We walked back to our mother's bedroom and knocked on the door. It took her a couple of minutes to open the door. When she finally did, she explained that she had fallen asleep because her hip had been hurting.

She was wearing a red long sleeve top with black pants, and the same black skullcap on her head from the evening before. She wore her black purse strapped around her neck and across her chest. She carried two worn plastic grocery bags, one in each hand. I am not sure what was in the bags, but as I glanced around inside of the home, I noticed pretty much all of the residents carried around their belonging in some type of old worn bag.

She pranced away from her bedroom with a great big smile on her face and led us into a huge dining room area. It had about ten very long tables with several chairs at each one. This was where the boarding home residents usually gathered to eat their meals, but we were the only people in there at that time. We placed the bags of food on one of the tables.

She mentioned that her hip was hurting and she had run out of pain pills. Grayson and Terrance offered to go to the store and buy her some and she accepted. She told them the brand she liked and asked for the large bottle of extra strength.

They left out of the house and headed to the store, while my mother and I remained seated in the dining area.

"Where is Devon?" she asked.

"He stayed back at the hotel to rest up for his early morning flight home," I responded.

There was a moment of silence, which I broke by asking a heartfelt question.

"Did you ever think about us over the years?"

She said, "Yes, all the time."

She mentioned again that she had ten children and told me she initially only wanted two children, a boy and a girl. She said, "If anybody would have told me I was going to have ten children, I would not have believed them!"

I felt surprised that she said that to me, because it brought up some feelings of rejection inside of me. However, I felt good knowing she was opening up to me. I was able to handle her truth.

At that moment, I remembered how my father would rant about how she did not want all of the children she was having. Yet, she did not believe in birth control or abortion. Hearing her say she never wanted so many children caused me to think about the adverse effect it must have had on her mental illness.

We avoided that subject when she asked me what I did for a living. I told her I had a regular full-time job and that I was an author of several books. I told her I began my writing journey by writing poems as a little girl. She smiled as she told me she used to write poetry when she was a little girl, too. She asked me what inspired me to become a writer. I told her that writing poetry helped me to deal with my feelings growing up.

I told her that everything I experienced as a child inspired me, like not knowing where she was and living in foster care after my father left.

"Is he still alive?" she asked.

I immediately remembered she had asked me that same question the day before; but I answered it as if it were the first time she asked.

"He passed away back in 1991," I told her.

"Are you sure?" she asked.

I told her that I was.

She said she could not believe he had passed away. She began telling me about the people upstairs on "the third floor" who have been saying that her "husband" was still alive.

I asked her "Which husband, Calvin or Father?"

She said my father.

Since she told me she and Calvin were married after leaving Kansas City, it was bizarre to me that she was still referring to *my* father, whom she left almost fifty years ago, as her husband. Furthermore, I knew that there was no "third floor" in the boarding home, so I presumed she was referring to the voices she hears in her head due to her mental illness.

With my brothers still being gone, I thought this might be a great time to ask her why she left.

"Do you remember anything about how things were just before you left Kansas City?" I asked.

She looked at me as if she was afraid to answer that question. She may have a mental illness, but she is very smart. I believe she was very aware that was a loaded question. I think we both knew that if she answered that question, it would lead to me wanting to know more about her time in Kansas City just before she left; In particular, why she left.

Therefore, instead of answering my question, she went back to talking about the people "upstairs."

Finally, my brothers returned from the store with her pain medicine. She took one of the pills right away, then we all sat around talking and eating.

A few minutes later, my niece called my phone number so that we could do a video call between our mother and my sister, Danisha. She entered the video and they were both smiling as they said hello to each other. All of a sudden, my sister asked, "Grace, how do you know this is our mother? She does not look like our mother." I felt speechless because I knew it would take more time than we had to explain how I knew she was our mother. To my surprise, our mother did not seem offended by my sister's doubt. She just asked her a couple of questions, which Danisha answered happily and they said their goodbyes.

My sister actually learned we had found our mother just moments before the video call. Therefore, she had not had the much-needed opportunity to process the information before being face-to-face with this estranged woman. The shocking news of finding our mother had been sprung on her without any prior preparation.

This left me feeling guilty that we had not told her sooner.

You see, we really wanted to take Danisha with us, however,

circumstances did not allow it. We made the difficult decision to travel without our sister with the intention of using technology to bring her together with the lady who delivered her into this world.

My father had once said, that out of all six of his children, he believed Danisha had the deepest affection for our mother. We did not know how the reunion would go and we did not want to subject her to any rejection if our mother did not receive us.

When our mother finally received us, we did not want to leave without giving Danisha an opportunity to see her and talk to her, since we did not know if or when we would ever be in-person with our mother again. Actually, my niece and I had discussed preparing my sister in advance of the video conversation. We had planned for her to arrive at my sister's place thirty minutes to one hour before the call. However, she arrived later than expected and did not get a chance to prep her mother for this very emotional interaction.

After our mother's chat with my sister, we kept on sitting in the dining area eating our meal and talking.

The worker who had met us at the door knew Geneva was our mother because we had announced it when we first arrived. She did not show a reaction at that time. But, she walked into the dining room with an extremely surprised look on her face.

She looked at Geneva and said, "You never told me anything about having children! I had no idea!"

Geneva looked at her but did not say anything.

The worker left the room and we continued to eat.

This was the second person who had expressed disbelief about Geneva having offspring. I was surprised to learn that denial was how my mother had chosen to cope with leaving all of her children. It seemed not having her children in her life had been difficult for her. It was hard for me to imagine how she must have felt about it. I wondered if maybe she had felt guilt, shame, or embarrassment. But, I did not dare ask her.

We continued to sit at the dining room table talking with our mother, with our chicken meal setting on the table. We had only bought enough food for our mother and ourselves, but we were not eating it very fast because we were spending a lot of time talking and learning more about our mother.

One of the boarding home residents came into the dining area, looked at our food and asked for some chicken. We gave her a piece. She left out of the room and came right back, looked at our food again and said, "I love mashed potatoes and gravy!" So, we gave her all the mashed potatoes and gravy we had left.

When a male resident saw her with the food, he came in and asked for some. Thankfully, we were able to honor his request.

I was very hungry but I had not eaten yet because I was busy conversing. I observed that there were two more pieces of chicken in the box, which I planned on eating when I got a break from talking. When I was finally ready to partake of some chicken, I looked in the box and it was empty.

Feeling puzzled, I looked around the table and none of my brothers had taken the chicken out of the box. Then I looked over to my right, at the table beside ours, and observed a male resident with a plate of chicken. He was eating it very fast and appeared to be enjoying it very much. I felt a little mystified because the box of chicken was sitting right in front of me, but I did not see the man take it.

I looked over to my left, at the table where my mother was sitting. My brother, Terrance, was standing in front of her. I had a baffled look on my face.

Terrance whispered, "I said he could take it."

The mystery was finally solved. I still felt hungry but I was happy the man was enjoying the chicken.

At that point, with the food being gone, I felt our visit would be over soon. So, I asked Grayson if he wanted to take a picture with our mother.

He said, "Yes."

I took one with my cell phone and one with his. Then I asked

Finding Mother: A Journey of Loss and Love

Grayson to use my cell phone to snap a picture of me with our mother. I had taken pictures of Jerome and Terrance with our mother the evening before, but not Grayson. As we were taking the pictures, again our mother mentioned feeling embarrassed about smiling due to the condition of her teeth.

Terrance told her that if she moved to Kansas City, it would be easy for us to take her to have her teeth fixed. We could monitor the process and take her to all of her appointments.

She reminded him of the "business" she has to take care of before she could consider moving.

After our photo session, we looked out of the window and noticed it was beginning to get dark. The descending darkness was a cue for us that we should go. As our visit was nearing its end, we all expressed to our mother how much we truly enjoyed our visit with her. We informed her how much we would love to bring her to live closer to us. We voiced our desire to remove her from the boarding home, move her to Kansas City and provide all of her needs. We reminded her that she had our phone numbers and that she could call us anytime.

One of the last things my brother, Terrance, said as we were walking out of the door was, "When you are ready to come to Kansas City just call and say, 'I wanna come.'"

She smiled and said, "Okay."

Each of us gave her a hug just before walking out of the door. When I gave her my goodbye hug, she kissed me on the jaw. Then we left out of the door.

The quarrel Terrance and I had gotten into before coming now seemed insignificant. He, Grayson, and I walked out together, jumped in our separate vehicles, drove back to the hotel, ate dinner, then retreated to our rooms to rest up for our flight back to Kansas City early the next morning.

As we traveled home, we shared our experience of meeting with mother. We all agreed on how nice it would be to bring her to live closer to us. We conversed about how we could place her in a safe environment, where people would not steal from her, where she would not have to carry all of her belongings around in a bag, where we could facilitate the treatment she needs for her hip pain, and where we could take her to have her teeth fixed.

We brainstormed about ways to keep the communication lines open with her and maybe inspire her to move closer when she felt more comfortable, after getting to know us better.

We all agreed it would be best for us to return home, call her every once in a while, send her cards and gifts for her birthday and other special occasions, with the hopes that we could bring her closer to us at a later date. We all realized that our hands were somewhat tied since that final decision would have to be hers. If she were happy to reside at the boarding home, then we should be happy, too.

Even though I agreed with my brothers, I still carried an unsettling feeling in my core. I left feeling disappointed because our mother did not readily accept our offers to move her to Kansas City, to allow us to provide a better life for her.

I was shocked that she preferred to stay in the poverty-stricken place she was living, when we could provide a nicer place. I know she said she had "business" to attend to before she could consider moving. However, I could not help but to wonder if she really had business or if that was just her way of stalling.

However, I had to realize that she had been living there for over fifteen years and while, to me, it looked like a bad place for her, to her it was home. Therefore, I had to accept her desires and just be grateful that I had this awesome chance to reunite with my mother.

The feeling of gratefulness in my heart matched the tenaciousness of my mind. If, by chance, she really did have "business," I felt determined to find out what it was and help her with it. I went back home thinking of ways to get her to move to Kansas City. I would not let what took place on this visit stop my efforts to bring Mother closer to her family.

Book Three

After the Reunion:
A Story of Acceptance

During the time period of this story, the author learned the diagnosis of her mother's mental illness. However, while she shared her symptoms, she made a personal decision not to share the actual diagnosis.

DEDICATION

To my daughter Arica. Thank you for traveling with me on that second visit to my mother. Your insight in helping me to communicate with her was awesome.

To my mother, "Geneva." Thank you for welcoming Arica and I when we came to visit you. I enjoyed listening as you recalled memories from your childhood and our family.

To the boarding home and behavioral health staff. Thank you for being so helpful and understanding. Your support, to my mother and us, was invaluable.

FOREWORD

As a little girl, knowing my mother's story, I felt sad that another child would grow up without a mother to take care of them.

Growing up, I observed closely every attempt my mother made to find Geneva. She even bought a book to learn how to be her own Private Investigator. Fueled by my mother's determination, I thought for certain that she would finally find her mother. Then after a failure too many, I would admit, "My mother will never find Geneva." All hope was lost. If Geneva were alive, we would have found a clue by now.

The day that my mother found Geneva I thought, "Finally, some good news!" I did not feel emotionally connected to my newly found grandmother. To me, my only grandmother was my father's mother. But, I was elated on my mother's behalf. She had spent the better part of her life searching for her. So, I hoped this would finally fill the void in her heart.

During the reunion, my mother called me after her first meeting with Geneva. Upon hearing that it was not going well, I felt a numbness. Thinking of my mother and uncles, I was disheartened. "She is going to hurt her children all over again, abandoning them for a second time."

The next day, I learned things were better. Happiness ensued. But, I could not understand why she acted the way she did the day before.

I went with my mother on her second visit to Geneva. The first time I met her, I realized the seriousness of her illness. Finally, I understood. I only hoped my mother would finally get the answers she deserved.

The *Finding Mother Series* will inspire readers to *feel* their feelings. It stirs people in similar situations to be at peace, but at the same time seek growth, in the midst of their circumstances.

~**Arica Miller, LMSW**
School Social Worker
Daughter of the author

Finding Mother: A Journey of Loss and Love

Finding Mother: A Journey of Loss and Love

INTRODUCTION

When I returned home after our very emotional reunion with our long-lost mother, there were *two* things I deeply desired: to learn why she had left, by hearing her talk about her side of the story, and to inspire her to move to Kansas City so my brothers and I could take care of her.

I experienced an array of feelings and emotions. I called my mother often and we would talk on the phone for many minutes. However, whenever the subject came up of why she left our family, she would either start talking about something else, or tell me about the things she was hearing from the "people on the third floor."

Likewise, whenever I tried to discuss her moving to Kansas City, so we could take care of her, she would say she had business to take care of before she could move. She would also say she could not talk about it because the boarding home workers were always listening to her phone conversations, and she did not want them to know what we were saying.

When I asked her if I could help her take care of her business, she said she could do it herself. When I reminded her of how I had always wanted to find her and take care of her, she said she takes care of herself. Eventually, I began to wonder if she really had "business," or if she was just trying to protect my feelings because she did not know how to tell me that moving closer to us, and allowing us to take care of her, was never in her plans.

Seeing as she was avoiding the two things I really wanted to discuss, I used the next few weeks as an opportunity to get to know her better. I was able to learn about her personality and sense of humor. I learned what she liked and what she loved. I noticed she never mentioned things she did not like. I learned that she did not talk about negative memories, only positive ones. It appeared to me she had suppressed all of her hurtful memories. In addition to learning things about her, I was able to send her cards and gifts every once in a while.

I also used the next few weeks to search for assisted living centers in my area. Even though I highly doubted she would really consider moving, I wanted to be sure that Kansas City offered some options. I really wanted to find my mother a place equipped to care for her mental health needs. It was a bit of a shot in the dark, but I desired to be prepared just in case, by chance, she took our offer seriously and decided to move closer to us.

Three months later, my mother was still no closer to Kansas City – and I was still no closer to the answers I desired. I was overjoyed at finally being able to speak with her on the phone – something I had never dreamed possible. But, all of those years of wanting her in my life left me with a longing for answers that could only come from her. I realized I needed to make a second trip.

This time I took my adult daughter with me. My daughter's involvement was crucial in helping my mother feel comfortable enough to give me the answers I desperately needed.

I call this "a story of acceptance" because I ultimately had to accept my mother's responses to my two most pressing concerns. I also had to accept some other things that I learned about her.

Chapter 1
RETURNING HOME AFTER THE REUNION

Besides still needing answers from my mother, when I returned home after the reunion, I continued to feel emotional. I also reached out again to Elsie, the caseworker at the Department of Children and Families, who had searched her database to see if my siblings were adopted through their agency.

A few days after the reunion, I took off work because I was not feeling well. While at home that day, I realized that part of the reason why I was not feeling well was because I was struggling with the way my mother was living.

I felt so downhearted that I sensed I needed someone trustworthy to talk to, to externalize my emotions. Because of the shock that came with finding my mother living in poverty, I had to be extra careful not to talk to just anyone. Most importantly I had to do it sooner rather than later.

After a meticulous online search, I found the number of a counseling hotline where I could speak with someone freely without revealing my true identity. When I called, a woman answered and I asked her if this was the type of line where I can have a counseling session with someone. She said it was not exactly counseling, but a line in which people talked and she listened. She said she could listen if I needed to talk.

Feeling like this was just what I needed, I asked, "So, I can start talking to you right now and you will listen?"

"Yes," she readily answered.

Realizing I finally had a golden opportunity to share what was on my heart concerning my mother, with someone who did not know me and therefore could not judge me, tears welled up in my eyes. I cried and began to talk about my feelings.

Finding Mother: A Journey of Loss and Love

I talked about how I found my mother after forty-nine years, and how I was not happy about the place she has been living. I expressed how my mother was living with beggars and peddlers who steal from her. I conveyed how I had always imagined I would find her in a mental hospital, locked up, maybe drugged up and not able to speak. I thought she would be in a safe environment, unlike where she was. She was living in a place where she has to pray for her safety every single day.

My mother is not supposed to be living under those impoverished conditions.

I had never imagined she would actually be able to speak, nor that she would be living in such disadvantaged surroundings.

I told the woman that, over the years before finding my mother, I had often thought of starting a homeless shelter that would accommodate anyone and everyone who needed a place to live, with no requirements and no expectations. They could just come get their needs met, be it food, a warm, dry place to lay their head for one night or a permanent place of shelter. Whenever I had those thoughts, I never imagined my own mother would be living in a similar environment.

Fortunately, she was not homeless.

She had been there for over fifteen years, so even though I did not like where she was living, she was surrounded by a stable environment, which she was content to call her home. Accepting this, I began to feel better about my mother's situation.

A sense of appreciation came over me as I realized I had actually come an extremely long way from having no idea where my mother was to finally finding her and talking with her!

The woman on the counseling hotline sensed I was feeling better. She had done a great job keeping quiet, and simply listening, while I vented. However, my story had sparked her interest. She asked my permission to ask me a couple of questions about the reunion to satisfy her curiosity.

I said, "Sure!"

Finding Mother: A Journey of Loss and Love

Her inquiry led to us conversing for another ten minutes after my emotions were content.

She admitted, "I am intrigued by your story. How did you finally find your mother?"

I told her, "It was a long, tedious journey, but I ultimately found her through an online people search."

"How did she feel about being found?" she asked.

I briefly told her the story of how, at first, she denied us then accepted us the next day after some prompting and prodding.

She said, "Wow! What a fascinating story!"

I felt impressed by her courage to ask me questions and I was happy to answer them. I appreciated her interest in my story.

I thanked her for listening to me and we said our good-byes. I hung up the phone feeling as if a very large weight had been taken away from me. With that burden lifted, I felt happy for the rest of the day and was able to return to work the next day feeling refreshed.

It was days after this "counseling" phone call that I began to spend more time on the phone with mother and sending her things.

Soon after that, I contacted Elsie again. Now that I had gotten my siblings names directly from my own mother, I remembered Elsie's generous offer. She had told me that if I ever learned my siblings' names, I should feel free to reach out to her again. I felt fortunate to know someone who had access to databases and was willing to help me anytime.

I emailed Elsie and told her I had finally found my mother after almost fifty years and that she was able to tell me the names of the children she had after leaving. I gave her the names and dates of birth for all four of the children and asked her if she would check to see if any of them were adopted through her agency. After I had sent the email, I sensed that with all the information I possessed that she was bound to find something this time. I felt very hopeful as I waited for her response.

Six days later, she emailed me back.

She was very excited that I had been reunited with my mother.

"Wow, that is amazing!! Hope it is going well as you two reconnect," she wrote, before thanking me for providing my siblings' information, and informing me that she would do everything in her power to help me. She said she would let me know the results of her search. I continued to feel hopeful as I anticipated what she would find.

While waiting for her response, I kept on trying to find an appropriate place for my mother to live, just in case, by chance, she actually decided to move to Kansas City to be closer to us.

Chapter 2
MY SEARCH FOR A PLACE FOR MOTHER

After the remarkable reunion, I continued to process my feelings about the condition in which I had found my mother. She said she used to walk outside a lot but not so much anymore for fear of being harmed. Therefore, my desire to provide for her became even stronger.

You see, ever since I was a little girl, I had always dreamed of finding my mother and taking care of her. Before reuniting with her, as soon as I knew we had located her, I began to think about moving her from where she was to where we were. Especially after the boarding home office manager, April, had warned us, before the reunion that we were not going to be happy when we saw her living conditions.

My mother was in her eighties, and had not received any family support for many years. Therefore, I assumed she should be more than ready to come and be with us, and allow us to take care of her.

So, I began discussing with April the type of facility I should be looking for in Kansas City that would meet her needs before we even saw our mother for the first time after so many years.

She explained to me that Geneva resided in an assisted living facility, in which they cook, clean, wash clothes, and manage medication for the residents. She had said that if I found a similar place in Kansas City, it would be seamless to transfer her from their facility to the new one. She told me to be sure to search for places that would accept my mother's source of income.

Yes, April had given me all the information I needed to begin searching for assisted living for my mother before we even reunited with her.

Finding Mother: A Journey of Loss and Love

After the reunion, I continued reviewing the benefits and amenities of numerous facilities. One of the first things I learned was that there is a difference between assisted living centers and nursing homes.

Assisted living centers cater to people who are able to take care of themselves, but who may need some assistance with daily living. Nursing homes cater to people who are not able to care for themselves, who need a higher level of care.

The assisted living facility where we found our mother is also known as a boarding home. One of the requirements for her to stay there was that she must attend *the center* daily, from early morning until late afternoon. "The center" is a mental health treatment center. All of the boarding home residents, including Geneva, receive transportation to and from there in a large blue bus every weekday.

The work of the center includes evaluating mental health patients, setting behavior goals, creating treatment plans and providing therapeutic activities. While there, Mother participates with group counseling, games and trips to the park. She also receives lunch and a snack and learns life skills.

In my search for an assisted living facility for her, a nurse told me that since she has a serious mental illness, she would also be eligible to live in a nursing home. However, my mother is very independent and when I visited nursing homes, the patients were severely handicapped and my mother is too independent to fit in with that environment. I ended up settling for two assisted living centers from which to choose. However, I was leaning more towards one in particular.

The first facility was located seventeen minutes away from my home and was set up like a large newer home. I liked that it was new and clean and that no more than twelve residents could live there at one time. An added plus to that was that all the rooms were located on one level. This would be ideal for my mother because she wouldn't have to climb stairs and strain her pained hip even more. As it happened, luck was on my side and they actually had two openings!

My mother would enjoy twenty-four-hour care, her own private room, and a private bathroom. She would also have meals prepared for her and someone to administer her medication daily. She could check out and go wherever she pleased. My first thought was that I could take her to places or even bring her to my home for visits if she wanted.

The second facility was located twenty-five minutes from my home and was an older building. It was very nice and clean, with a forty-residents limit. They actually had a couple of vacancies on the first floor. This facility had the same benefits as the other one, and then some more.

In addition to caretakers, it had a round-the-clock nurse, security, and a doctor who visits on site. My mother would have a psychiatrist who actually comes to her on location to monitor her mental illness and medications. She would even receive treatment and physical therapy for her hip right there on site!

The second facility also featured a chapel for Sunday morning worship, so my mother could attend if she wanted. There was a beauty salon, so she could have her hair washed and styled regularly. In addition, a full-service nursing home was attached to the assisted living home. Therefore, if my mother ever became unable to care for herself, she could move directly over to the nursing home without us having to find a new place for her to live.

After visiting both places, I liked the second one best. I requested a packet of information to share with my brothers, with hopes of having an opportunity to share it with my mother during my second trip. That way she would see for herself how much we wanted her and that we would do anything to have her in our lives once again.

Chapter 3
A TYPICAL PHONE CALL WITH MOTHER

As time passed, my phone calls with mother became more frequent. Initially, we would talk once a month, but after a short while, we would be on the phone every other week. Sometimes, we spoke again after only a few days. Mother was a regular thought in my mind so I was often thinking about what I could do for her, be it talking on the phone, mailing her a package, or researching living facilities.

Whenever we would talk on the phone and I would ask her if she needed anything, she always let me know what she needed. Whenever I sent her things, she was always happy to receive them. In fact, she would remind me of holidays that were coming up, which I liked.

The first time I called her after we got home from reuniting with her she told me, "You know Mother's Day is coming up on the 13th of May?" In a later phone conversation, she reminded me of her birthday and Christmas.

Almost a year later, when Valentine's Day was two weeks away, she said to me, "You know Valentine's Day is coming up?" When I told her that I sent her a Valentine's Day gift, she told me, "I love surprises!" Her reminders let me know what occasions were important to her, so, I made sure to send her gifts for each one of them.

When she would remind me of those special dates, I felt happy that she was comfortable doing so. It filled my heart with joy. I liked that she was able to open up with me and communicate exactly what was important to her. I also felt honored that she was willing to accept gifts from me. Overall, I felt pleased that she was mentally able to express herself in this way because this meant I did not have to go through the trouble of inquiring about what she wants and needs to the boarding home workers. It was my great pleasure to provide anything she desired.

Most of the time, our conversations were just random chatting. Whenever I would call and speak to her, the ritual would go like this:

"May I speak to Geneva?"

The boarding home worker would reply, "Just a moment. Geneva! Your daughter is on the phone! Somebody go tell Geneva her daughter is on the phone."

Then usually two to four minutes later a, now familiar, voice would inquire on the other side of the phone, "Hello?"

A huge smile would break up on my face before regaining my composure enough to say, "Hello, Mother, how are you doing?"

"Oh, so-so, my hip has been hurting."

Quite often she would ask questions like, "What have you been doing?" or "Did you do anything fun today?"

That would be the only urge I would need to tell her all about my day and my writing.

Each time, the topic varied, because the turn of our conversation would depend on her follow-up questions like, "Did you go to church today?" "Do you still go to Sunday School?" "Have you talked to Carla?" or "How is Terrance doing?"

When I called her on the Fourth of July, she asked me if my church was doing anything special that day.

I told her my church has never celebrated the Fourth of July.

She told me that when she was little girl, her church *always* celebrated *every* holiday, and that her church would have cookouts at the park. She often asked the same questions in our current conversation that she asked in our past conversations. I always enjoyed answering all of her questions.

It seemed she was asking me those questions for a few reasons. The first, she may have appreciated me calling her and she enjoyed talking to me. The second, she could have wanted me to feel like she really wanted to talk to me, especially since a lot of the time she would prefer to be in her bed resting her hip. A third, she might have been aiming towards being kind to her daughter whom she knew loved her.

Even with her mental illness, I believe she recognized that she could possibly sadden me if it appeared she did not want to be bothered with me. Remembering my responses to her questions was a sign, to me, that she enjoyed hearing them. I felt intrigued whenever she would inquire, in a later conversation, about something we discussed in a prior one.

During our phone conversations, I usually asked her if she had received any package that I may have sent, and if she liked it. She usually liked everything.

She would tell me about the weather in her city. She would say, "It is cold here!" or "It is hot like a furnace outside!"

Oftentimes, she would talk about the center that she attends daily, telling me what they served for lunch, which was usually something she really liked. She would inform me about the special meals, like when the center served Thanksgiving dinner, or the boarding home had a cookout and served barbecue for the Fourth of July.

Sometimes, when she would want to get off the phone, but wanted to avoid hurting my feelings, she pretended the boarding home workers needed to use the phone. I remember one time vividly.

We were in the middle of a conversation when Mother's voice went distant from the receiver and I heard her saying, "Do you need to call that lady who called earlier?"

I frowned down on my phone. "Mother, do you need to get off the phone?"

"I think so. You see, a woman called earlier and I think they want to call her back."

I was feeling torn between continuing our conversation and letting her go. "Do they need you to get off the phone?"

"No!" I heard one of the workers proclaim from the background. "Nobody needs to use the phone. She wants to get off the phone, but she is trying to blame us."

Mother released an embarrassing chuckle.

"Mother, they are telling on you."

"Yeah," she said, before letting out another quiet laugh.

In that moment, I experienced a series mixed thoughts.

Should I feel sad about her trying to be sneaky about getting off the phone? Does she not want to talk to me? If she needs to go, why don't she just say so?

"Mother, I can let you go. I like to call you every once in a while, to see how you are doing and to let you know I am thinking about you. You don't have to stay on the phone for a long time, unless you want to. Do you need to get off the phone?"

Mother humbly replied, "It's okay. So, what have you been doing?

Then after a few more words back and forth, she said, "Well, I want to go lay in my bed and rest a little."

I said, "Okay, it was very nice talking to you."

"It was nice talking to you, too."

"Have a nice rest of the day," I told her.

"Thank you. You, too."

"Okay, bye."

She said, "Bye."

After that call ended, memories flooded back of all of the other times when Mother did that same thing, but the workers never clearly told on her that way. She just succeeded in getting off the phone.

During our talks, I learned some fun facts about her. She loves cookies and banana pudding. She loves desserts in general. She enjoys telling stories about herself when she was growing up. When she was a little girl, she really enjoyed licking the cake and cookie batter out of the bowl after her mother would fill the baking pans.

Finding Mother: A Journey of Loss and Love

Our conversations usually consisted of the same types of dialogue each time. I cannot say I blame her for preferring to be by herself rather than talking on the phone. After all, she had been to herself for many, many years, with no family. So, getting phone calls from her children was something new for her, something she had to get used to.

I actually felt disappointed and took it personally at the first indication that she did not feel like talking when I would call, especially since I truly desired for her to open up and tell me why she left us. Also, I really needed to know her true feelings about allowing us to move her to Kansas City. Therefore, a second trip to visit Mother became more and more appealing.

Chapter 4
MY SECOND TRIP TO VISIT MOTHER

The need for answers to my burning questions was so potent that I made a second trip to visit my mother. This time, I planned to take my daughter, Arica, with me. I needed a travel partner, and I thought this would be a great opportunity for her to meet her grandmother. Arica is a Licensed Social Worker and so her expertise came in handy during our trip in a way I never expected.

Leading up to my second trip, mother acted very excited about our coming. Whenever I would call her, she would ask, "Are you and Arica still coming? June 7th, right?" Every time one of my brothers called her, she would ask them, "Are Grace and Arica still coming on June 7th?" I felt happy about her being excited to see us and could not wait for her to meet Arica.

There were several things I wanted to do together during our trip and I discussed my expectations with my mother over the phone.

I asked her, "Would you allow me to take you out to dinner during our visit?"

She said, "Yeah. That would be okay."

"Also, I would like to show you some information about a couple of assisted living facilities that I have in mind for you. I understand you may never decide to move, but I just wanted to give you something tangible to think about."

She said, "Yeah. That would be okay, too."

I could not bottle up my final expectation any longer. I told her that when we are in person during our visit, that I wanted her to tell me why she left. I felt my breath catch in my throat and the moment her voice affirmed that it would be okay, I felt overwhelmed.

She agreed to all of my requests, so I felt increasingly excited about our visit and could not wait. Even though I knew she probably would not agree to move, I was extremely hopeful. I was even prepared to bring her back in the car with us if she agreed to it. Admittedly, my hopes were up way too high, but that did not stop me from remaining highly optimistic. I really wanted my mother to live closer to us. I often imagined how great it would be for her to be in Kansas City, to meet all of her grandchildren; and for all of us to throw a big dinner just to celebrate her.

Although I really wanted to bring my mother back to be closer to us, I knew I could not do it by myself. I needed my brothers' support that they so amply provided. When Arica and I were making our plans, my brother, Terrance, pitched in some cash to help us pay for the trip. Our hope was that I would use the trip to convince our mother to move to Kansas City. We really, really wanted her near us, to make her happy by providing for all of the things she needed and wanted. Our biggest hope was to be able to give her the life we felt she deserved. Therefore, this trip would not be just for fun and enjoyment. We were on a true mission!

As Arica and I continued to prepare for the trip, we decided we would drive a rental car. It would be a seventeen-hour drive, but we estimated that it would take us at least a day to get there, with all the stops for food and rest. We agreed on a hotel that was only a ten-minute drive from the boarding home where my mother lived. The hotel we chose provided free continental breakfast so that would save us some time and money.

While packing, I started thinking about our prior visit when we reunited with Mother. I remembered the great effect that the family photos I had taken with me had on her ability to recall memories of her life before leaving us so many years earlier. I remembered the sincere interest she had shown in the photos and how much she had enjoyed them.

During our reunion visit, I noted that the more she looked at the pictures, the more it began to "click" for her that we were her children. The more she realized we were her children, the more she opened up, and eventually accepted us. To say that the pictures were a powerful tool would be an understatement. However, during our initial reunion visit, I had run out of pictures to show her and I wished I had brought more.

For this second trip Arica and I were preparing for, I sorted through my many albums, pulled out as many photos as I thought she would appreciate and packed them up. I even took a little album, full of pictures of herself and her adopted family, that our cousin had given me to show her. Our cousin believed that those pictures would help jog her memory.

I was thrilled to be able to take so many because I knew she didn't have any. With all the moving around, and her health being such as it is she had lost every tangible memory of her family.

Initially, we had planned to leave on the morning of Thursday, June 8th. However, the rental car company informed us that we could pick the car up after five o'clock the evening before without any additional fee. That opportunity moved things forward and we decided to take advantage of it and get on the road that very evening. My brother, Jerome, was concerned, because he didn't like the idea of our having to drive through the night on unfamiliar roads.

He urged us to leave early the next morning so that our travel would be mostly daytime hours. Even though I understood his concern, the thought of getting on the road as soon as possible appealed to me. I felt like the sooner we were on our way the sooner we would reach our destination. Arica and I discussed it, and she was all for getting a head start. We packed our suitcases and plenty of healthy snacks, picked up our rental car, and drove straight to the highway!

One of the most remarkable things about our twenty-four-hour road trip was that my oldest brother, Jerome, contacted us every so often to make sure we were safe. He encouraged us not to sleep in the car at rest stops, but to book a hotel instead.

As the main driver, I was perfectly capable of functioning with only a few hours of sleep, so checking into a hotel seemed excessive to me. In the end, Arica and I decided to chance it and slept in the car in well-lit large convenient store parking lots, whenever we stopped to get gas. Each time after we would wake up, I bought a cup of coffee to help me keep awake until the next time we would stop. Even though we did not do as my brother suggested, his phone calls and texts were very welcomed. I felt like he really cared about us, and that alone was the only sense of security I needed.

During the trip, Arica and I talked, laughed and listened to music. I was happy because that was a chance to bond with my daughter. A special opportunity to spend time together.

My most memorable experience, during our drive there, was enjoying the variety of healthy snacks that Arica prepared. She had brought along several soft, perfectly ripe avocados and a loaf of fresh bread.

On one of our stops along the way, she peeled and removed the seeds from three or four of the avocados, put the edible portion in a clear glass bowl and mashed it with a fork.

She added salt and pepper and stirred to her desired consistency. Then took a slice of bread in one hand and a fork in the other. My daughter dipped the fork into the bowl, which sat on her lap atop of the blanket and pillow that was keeping her warm and comfortable throughout the drive.

When she had just the right portion of the avocado mixture on the fork, she spread it on to the slice of bread.

I watched intensely as she completed the task.

As I stared, she stretched her arm towards me with the prepared avocado snack sitting on her hand. "This one is for you," she said.

I felt honored and joyful to receive it. My daughter's avocado bread had always been one of my favorite finger foods.

Then she made one for herself.

As I was biting into the delicious snack that my daughter had so carefully prepared, I thought about how grateful I felt that

Finding Mother: A Journey of Loss and Love

finding my mother had resulted in my sharing this special moment together with my daughter.

Several times we stopped for gas, food, and to get some rest. We enjoyed our journey, taking our time and not being in a rush. We were careful to stay within the speed limit throughout the entire trip, until finally reaching our destination. I did most of the driving but as we got closer, Arica took the wheel and drove us the final way. After we got off the highway in my mother's city, traffic was very congested.

I felt relieved to finally arrive, but I felt nervous in the high-volume traffic.

The people who were driving on the road around us seemed unconcerned about other drivers or common safety rules. Whenever we had the right of way, the other drivers did not yield to allow us to have it. Driving in that city was clearly different from Kansas City. In the end, we just allowed everyone to pass us by because it would earn us nothing but a headache, not to mention that it would sour our anticipation and good mood.

It had been twenty-four hours since we had started our trip, and now we were weaving our rental car through the somewhat familiar roads leading to our hotel. I felt relieved as we entered the parking lot, walked into the hotel and strolled over to the front desk to check in. This meant we were that much closer to finally spending time with my mother.

Finding Mother: A Journey of Loss and Love

Chapter 5
ARRIVING ON THURSDAY EVENING

It was around five o'clock in the evening of June 7th when we left Kansas City; and it was around five o'clock in the evening of June 8th when we arrived at our out-of-town hotel. Arica and I were both tired and felt like resting, but I was too excited and wanted to go see my mother right away.

The anticipation of driving to the boarding home where she lived was intense. The thought of getting back into the car and driving on the hectic roads was not appealing to me, though.

The last time I went to the boarding home, I was with my brothers, but this time, I was going to be with my daughter. I was concerned about returning to that rundown and unkempt neighborhood without the company of strong men. Would we feel safe?

Would Arica and I be able to sit inside long enough to truly enjoy our visit with the foul odor that seemed to fill every corner of that boarding home?

Even with those concerns, this was my mother and she was worth any inconvenience that I would experience just to see her, talk to her, and finally get the answers to my two pressing concerns.

I knew my mother did not know the exact time we were coming. I had called the boarding home several times but either the line stayed busy or no one answered the phone. Therefore, I had no other way of letting my mother know when to expect us. I knew she had been excited about us coming. I just hoped she would be prepared for our visit when we showed up.

After we had settled in at the hotel, we freshened up and left to go see my mother. Twenty minutes later, my daughter and I entered the building. In my hands, I was clutching the small bag containing all the photos I had so meticulously collected.

Finding Mother: A Journey of Loss and Love

After taking a moment to adjust to the odor, we headed for the office. We told the worker we were there to see my mother, Geneva. She sent one of the residents to get her.

While waiting for Mother to enter the room, I asked, "Is April here? She is the person who I spoke to on the phone when I finally located my mother after so many years, and I have wished to meet her in person." The worker responded, "I am sorry, she is not here. She will not be back into the office again until next week." Feeling a sense of disappointment, I knew meeting April was not something that was going to happen during this trip.

When my mother came to greet us, she had a big smile on her face and seemed very happy to see us. She was carrying a very large black backpack in one of her hands. I immediately remembered that the last time I visited her, she was carrying around two plastic grocery bags. By the looks of it, she had graduated to a backpack and it appeared she was carrying around a lot more stuff now than what she had toted in the bags.

I wondered if it was because I had been sending her things, so now she had more belongings to carry around. She told us during our first visit that when she leaves things in her bedroom, other residents steal it. She really enjoyed receiving things from me and my brothers. Although I liked sending her things, I carried some guilt about the fact she had to carry it everywhere she went. I felt sad because the more I sent, the more she had to carry around. It was simply wrong. That was not how things were supposed to be for a person in her state and age.

That was yet another thing that sparked my already strong desire to take her out of that place and move her to Kansas City. She would be so much better in a safe facility where she could leave her stuff in her room without the fear of it being stolen.

After going in for a great big hug and a kiss on Mother's cheek, I took one tiny step back, and looked at the beautiful young lady that had traveled with me.

Finding Mother: A Journey of Loss and Love

"This is my daughter, Arica, your Granddaughter!" I said to Geneva with a proud-like excitement. Gleaming, she looked at Arica's face, then, looked at my face, as if to see there was any resemblance.

Arica fixed her eyes on Mother's face. "Wow, it is wonderful to finally meet you!"

"It is nice to meet you, too," Mother smiled.

"It is amazing how much my mother favors you."

They both were smiling.

It gave me a feeling of sheer gratefulness to finally have the honor of introducing them.

She invited us to sit in the large living room area. The living room featured brown hardwood floors, an old non-functional fireplace, a large television mounted on the wall, two long couches, and some chairs.

The couches were dirty. The odor was unbearable, yet familiar. It filled the home during our initial reunion visit. But, we all were so caught up with the tension of the reunion that the odor seemed insignificant. Smelling it at the second visit made me feel saddened because I was thinking we could provide her a much better living environment, if only she would accept our offer.

Overall, the living room was organized, the walls were free of flaws, and the floor was clean.

There was a door in the living room that led to the office area. The top half of the office door was opened while the bottom half remained shut. I presumed this was to keep boarding home residents from entering the office. I saw a worker in there.

The television was on, turned up loud and showing a movie. About four or five residents were sitting in the living room watching it. My mother, Arica and I did not really talk about anything significant since the noise prevented us from having a meaningful conversation. However, I showed my mother some of the pictures I had brought and she seemed to be enjoying them very much. Her interest was especially piqued by the ones of my oldest sister, Carla, and those of herself when she was a little girl.

During our first reunion visit, I had given her my only copy of an Army picture of my sister, Danisha. When I went back home, I wished I had taken a copy of the picture with my cell phone. So, now that I was in person with my mother again, I asked her if she still had the picture and if it would be possible for me to snap a photo on my mobile phone.

"Yes," was all she answered and she stood up and left the living room, heading for the direction of her bedroom.

While she was gone, I kept looking towards the direction she went, watching for her return. Five minutes later, the familiar feeling of abandonment consumed me and I feared she wouldn't be coming back. Lifting myself off the couch, I went to her room and knocked lightly on the locked door. As I was waiting for her to open, I had an awful feeling, like she was never going to open it.

Finally, she opened the door and came out of the room with the picture in hand. I was relieved, as the few moments that I waited outside of the door seemed like an hour. She looked at me as if to wonder why I could not wait.

Suddenly, I felt embarrassed for my irrational feelings, but mostly surprised by my reaction. I was wondering what had come over me because normally I would have been able to wait with no problem. I was afraid she might be offended by my inability to wait for her to return. However, seeing the considerate look on her face, it was like she actually understood. We went back into the living room and sat on the couch with Arica.

As my mother continued to enjoy the pictures, I was still dwelling on how I had experienced fear that my mother was not going to come back when she went to her bedroom to get the picture. I was wondering if I had reverted back to the two-year-old abandoned toddler who wanted her mother to come back, but she never returned. I wondered if what I was experiencing was a fear of being abandoned by my mother for a second time.

Finding Mother: A Journey of Loss and Love

In analyzing the situation, I recalled three instances when I was three and four years old, and felt afraid of being abandoned by my grandmother. She babysat me while my father worked after my mother had left.

The first instance was when my grandmother took me to her niece's house to leave me while she ran some errands. I refused to go to her niece because I had this notion that if I went to her, my grandmother would walk out and never come back.

The second instance was when my grandmother took me to a daycare center to leave me there for a few hours. Once again, the exact same thing happened. I refused to go with the daycare worker for fear of never seeing my grandmother again.

The last incidence was when grandmother led me to the kindergarten for the first time. I remember being terrified that if I would turn my back and sit down with the rest of the children, she would leave and never return.

In each of those instances, I witnessed my grandmother hesitating to leave, by hiding behind walls and peeping around corners until I was finally distracted enough for her to sneak away.

I finally finished analyzing that awkward situation and brought my thoughts back into the current moment. I noticed my mother was looking closely at one of the pictures from the album my cousin had sent. It was a picture of her standing in front of her childhood home. She quoted the address and stared at that picture much longer than any of the other ones.

Intrigued by the way she was gazing at the photo, I asked her what it was about that picture that she could not take her eyes off it.

"That's me!" she said.

I felt surprised that of all the pictures I had shown her of herself, she liked that one the most. That one was not a close-up like some of the other ones, nor were her facial features as clear. Nevertheless, that one captured her heart.

As she continued to look at the small photo album, she recognized a picture of my grandmother's husband.

"That looks like my uncle who raised me," she said.

I told her that was him. Then she grinned as she talked about how she used to comb his hair, when he had hair. He had a bald head in the picture. Since she was enjoying the pictures in that album more than I expected, I told her she could keep the entire album. My cousin predicted those pictures would jog her memory and she was right!

After the high I was feeling while watching her enjoying herself with those pictures, a calm nervousness engulfed me. We were having such a great time, but I suddenly remembered my main reasons for being there.

It dawned on me that I was sitting right beside the woman who I needed answers from. I felt like it was now or never. I was thinking that when we took her out to dinner, I would ask her to tell me her story about why she had left. That would be the right way to pursue the issue since I believed she would be able to talk freely away from the prying ears of her housemates.

Therefore, I used this moment to seek her true intentions about moving to Kansas City.

I asked her if she had thought any more about moving to live closer to us. She looked over at the office area as if she could not answer because the office workers would be nosey and listen to our conversation.

She said, "I can't talk here."

I asked her if she wanted to go into another room or outside.

I told her I really needed to know and would respect whatever her answer may be. Understanding this, she told me that when she first moved into the boarding home, fifteen years ago, it was in way worse condition.

She said they had done many nice things to the house, like fixing major holes in the walls and painting. She explained that she was used to being there. Furthermore, she expressed that she did not want to leave at this time.

Although I was saddened, I understood how she felt, and most of all, I truly appreciated her honesty.

I knew I had a packet full of assisted living information out in the car, but was afraid to show it to her since we obviously would not be bringing her to live in Kansas City anytime soon.

My brother Terrance and I had discussed leaving the information with her so she would at least have something tangible to look at and think about. However, my optimism had faded and I felt afraid to mention it to her after she had made her intentions clear. I said nothing about it and let it stay in the car.

My daughter and I saw that it was getting dark outside. We had planned on going to a restaurant for dinner before it got too late. I asked my mother if it was okay for us to visit her at the center the next day.

She said, "Yes. Nobody has ever visited me there before, but that will be okay." She told us that Friday would be finger nail polish day.

We hugged, said our good-byes, and returned to our hotel.

That night, I spoke with Terrance on the phone to get his opinion about whether I should have shown our mother the assisted living information, since she had clearly indicated not wanting to move.

He insisted that I *should* have and instructed me to leave it with her so she could at least have something tangible to contemplate. Since we sacrificed the time and resources to travel all the way there just for the opportunity to try to convince her, we could not give up now. Besides me wanting to talk to her about why she left, the entire purpose of the visit was to try to win her over to bring her to Kansas City.

This was our only shot at giving her the information. We knew that once I was back home, it would be impossible to have that type of discussion with her. We had to take advantage of the up close and personal opportunity that I had with her while I was there.

Based on Terrance's counsel, I planned to take the information and talk with her about it when we visited her the next day. We ended our conversation.

Arica and I shared our thoughts about how the evening had gone before we retired to our beds for a good night's sleep. As I dozed off that night, I felt like we had a great time with my mother. I truly enjoyed the first day of our visit and I could not wait to wake up to the second.

Chapter 6
DAY TWO OF OUR VISIT - FRIDAY

I woke up the next morning, envisioning the fun we would have sitting in the center, participating in activities with my mother. Then I started thinking about the two specific purposes I had for going back again to visit my mother. I would wait until Sunday to ask her about why she left her family so many years ago. I longed to know her story.

However, today, I knew that I had to show her the assisted living information that I brought. I knew I would need to leave it with her so that she could have something to ponder over after we left. I was feeling grateful for Terrance inspiring me to go ahead and give her the packet of information.

My mother had told Arica and I to come to the center around noon. So, we ate an early lunch at a downtown restaurant before going. When we arrived at the address, we met the center manager, Donna, outside as we approached the door of the building. She asked if she could help us find something. I told her we were looking for the center. She told us we were at the right place, but seemed puzzled about what we were doing there. After all, most of the people who attend the center do not have families or visitors.

I told her I was Geneva's daughter and that my siblings and I had found her after forty-nine years.

She expressed a variety of feelings.

"Oh my, I am so excited that the two of you are here! This is a surprise! I never even knew Geneva *had* children! It is amazing that you were able to find your long-lost loved one after so many years."

She graciously invited us into the building. We walked up two flights of stairs to arrive at the front door of the center. As we stood outside of the that door, Donna was still in shock that we were actually there.

Finding Mother: A Journey of Loss and Love

"I am so delighted that you all came! Most of the mental health patients who attend our center do not have anyone who cares about them. So, we are *always* in support of families who are concerned and want to be involved."

I told her of my desire to move my mother to Kansas City to be closer to us, and of my intent to try to woo her into considering it.

She said she would do anything in her power to help my siblings and me. Then, she gave me her cellular phone number and told me I was welcome to call her anytime. She told me that her and my mother joked around with each other a lot, but she did not really know a lot about her personal life because my mother tends to be private.

She also told me my mother had a mental illness and that, as long as she took her medication, she was nice and did not bother anyone. She mentioned they recently had some difficulty getting her to take it consistently. She told me a story of how the workers noticed she had been acting angry and cussing at people more than usual.

The staff came up with a bright idea to check under the mattress on her bed. There they found the pills she was supposed to be taking daily, but she had been hiding them instead. Donna said she had to remind my mother that if she did not take her medication that she could end up locked up in a mental hospital again. Having a fear of going back there, she started taking it regularly.

There seemed to be a consensus among all of the workers that she "was nice, quiet, and does not bother anybody." Donna said the thing that impressed her the most about Geneva is she resides around drugs all day, every day in the boarding home, but she will not touch them.

I felt very amazed and grateful to hear that my mother had no interest in using drugs.

I told her I was looking forward to joining my mother in the center activities. However, she explained that the center was a mental health treatment center. Therefore, to maintain the privacy of the patients, outsiders were not allowed to enter. I felt a little let down and kind of embarrassed for expecting to participate, not knowing it was private. She invited us to sit down in the lobby area while she went in to get Geneva.

With her backpack in hand, Geneva came walking out, with a cheerful grin on her face. She sat down in a chair. She seemed very happy that we were there.

For a moment, I was feeling a little guilt, like we were causing her to miss the center activities. Then I realized the staff probably felt like visiting with her long-lost family may be more therapeutic to her than participating with the center for that day. Besides, she goes to the center every day, but it is rare for family to visit.

Just then, Donna came out of the center door with a very happy-for-Geneva type of look on her face and asked, "Geneva, who are these people?"

Not realizing we had already told Donna who we were, my mother told her that it was none of her business.

Donna asked, "Is this your daughter and your granddaughter?"

My mother looked surprised realizing Donna already knew who we were. She did not answer.

I felt embarrassed for my mother because I knew she had been living in denial about having children for forty-nine years. I knew she had not revealed to anyone that she had children. She seemed like she was pleased to have us there, but was not so proud of herself for having kept her very painful past a secret for so long.

After that very uncomfortable moment was over, my mother looked over at us and asked us how our morning had been. As I was telling her about our morning, I noticed her fingernails, freshly polished with a shiny reddish-orange polish. She asked if I had heard from Carla. I told her I had not and reminded her that my sister was still missing.

Chapter 7
DAY TWO OF OUR VISIT – TALKING WITH MOTHER

"Do you know where Carla's husband is?" Mother inquired. I told her Carla did not have a husband. She never married.

"Carla took the role as my parental figure for six years.

"After Daddy had left us in that house alone when I was seven, landing us in foster care, he regained full custody of us three years later. The first two years after he had gotten us back, he took us with him whenever he traveled. He was determined to never leave us again.

"Devotedly, he sat in the audience when Carla walked across the stage to get her high school diploma at age seventeen. He stood up and screamed, 'Go Carla!' That surprised me because he did not usually do things like that. He was so proud of her.

"He did his best to stay with us. That is, until Carla turned eighteen. Jerome, Grayson and Terrance were in the military. Daddy began traveling again, without us. This time, leaving Danisha and me to live with Carla, who was now a legal adult. I lived with her from ages twelve through seventeen.

"She was kind of like a mother to me. I had to ask for her permission to go places. My big sister would say, 'You can go after you clean up that kitchen.'

"I would beg to wear her clothes and shoes.

"She would say, 'No, they are too big for you.'

"I would plead with her until, finally, she would say, 'Go ahead and wear them.'"

We all laughed.

Arica asked, "Oh, did you know that my mom was homecoming queen at her high school?"

My mother said, "Oh. You were?"

"Yes, I was Football Homecoming Queen," I said.

Mother laughed.

Then she remembered how when she was in grammar school, the boys and girls who sold the most cookies were crowned king and queen. She remembered that the homecoming ceremony was celebrated on May Day, of each year. She said her school had relay races first thing in the morning. "Then in the evening we had May Day," she recalled.

I asked her what grade she went to in school.

She said she went to the twelfth grade.

"But I was in a different place back then," she said.

"What place were you in?" Arica asked.

She told Arica the name of the city and state she was in back then. I was impressed with the way Arica asked her for clarification at a moment when I was wondering what "a different place" meant, but had not thought to ask.

I asked my mother if she went to college.

She said, "No. I just finished school, that's all."

I asked her how old she was when she first got married.

She said, "I was twenty. I had just got my first job."

I asked her what she did at her first job and she said she hung up coats and put them in place.

Then she continued her story, "So after I got my job, I worked there for two years. Then that's when I met my husband. There was a girl who worked at the same place where I worked. So, she asked me 'You want to come over my sister's house with me?' I said, 'Yeah, I'll go.' So, at her sister's house, that is where I met my husband."

She told me that she and my father moved to another state where he got a job, and they lived there for about eight years. One day he told her he had to go to Arizona for work.

She said, "So, he traveled around all over, you know, to get a job. Sometimes he would leave me there, sometimes about a week and sometimes about two weeks before he would come back."

Finding Mother: A Journey of Loss and Love

Keeping my emotions bottled up was impossible. "Wow!" I exclaimed as the reality of that truth weighed on me.

I knew my father had left my five siblings and me in a house alone so that he could go work in Florida. But, I never knew that was something he often did before my mother left. When he left my siblings and me in that house alone, when I was seven, I thought it was the first time he had done such a thing.

Arica asked, "What was it about him that you decided to marry him?"

This question made us all laugh.

I think my mother was actually blushing as she explained, "Oh, he was nice and he was always helpful to me." She continued, "Yeah, he was nice to me and the kids, and like I said, he worked out of town, you know. And his boss would send him different places. When you're doing cement finishing, as soon as they would finish on one job, he'd go to another one. His boss would give him a job someplace else. Just on and on, we traveled around for a while. I liked the places he took me. Yeah uh huh."

Arica asked her which child she gave birth to first, Devon or Carla?

She said, "Devon," referring to my older brother Jerome, whom she called by his middle name.

"And after that you had Carla?" Arica asked.

"No, Grayson was number two. I wanted a girl. But, it didn't come as a girl. It came as a boy. I said, 'Another boy?'" she laughed. "So, then I had Carla."

I asked her if she was happy that she had her girl.

She said, "Yeah."

We all laughed.

She smiled, "I had my girl. She was as cute as a button."

Then mother looked at me and said, "You were the last one. Grace was the last one."

I asked her if she remembers having me.

She smiled and said, "Yeah."

Finding Mother: A Journey of Loss and Love

Still talking about me, she continued, "She was a real fat baby. She was the cutest thing you ever want to see."

Then she said Terrance was born after Carla.

I asked, "And then Danisha?"

She said, "Yeah."

While talking about the birth order of the children she and my father had together, she tried to quote my birthplace, Terrance's birthplace, and Danisha's birthday. She quoted them all wrong. Then she said, "I had everything written down. But, after my stuff was stolen, it was misplaced, I had to write it all down again. Grace was the last one. She was bad, too!"

We all laughed.

I clarified, "You said she was bad?"

She said, "Yeah."

I joked, "That hasn't changed."

We all laughed.

Sometimes, it seemed like my mother did not realize she was actually talking to me when she recalled memories about "Grace." I found that intriguing. I asked her if she remembered walking me to a convenience store in Kansas City.

She said, "No."

Mother often answered with one word.

"Do you remember walking to the store and taking me with you? My brothers and sisters would be at school and Daddy would be at work. You would buy me chocolate covered malt balls and the clerk would hand them to me."

I laughed as I told her how, for years, I had been sharing the story of how the store clerk would *give* me malt balls. Later realizing that *she* had actually paid for the candy and the clerk was merely *handing* it to me.

"Malt balls are my favorite candy to this day because of that."

She said, "Oh yeah?"

I said, "Yeah."

Finding Mother: A Journey of Loss and Love

Then I told her I remembered going into the closet, in her and my father's bedroom, trying to put on her clothes and shoes.

Mother did not seem to think that story was funny. In fact, she looked agitated when I was talking about putting on her clothes and shoes. Seeing the disturbed look on her face made me feel like this could be an example of why she said I was "bad." I do remember her picking me up taking me away from her closet and as soon as she was not looking, I went right back in.

To lighten the moment, Arica asked her which city was her favorite of all the cities she had been to. She said it was the outskirts of Los Angeles, California.

She explained, "We lived in a suburban area. And uh, it never got too cold and it never got too hot. It was pleasant all the time in that area. But, up in the mountains of Los Angeles, there was snow. We never had snow."

Arica asked her how she ended up in her current city and state.

"Oh, I had a friend that came here and he brought me along."

Then she digressed to talking about a job she had at a toy manufacturing company while she and my father were together. "I got a job so I could help bring some money in." She recalled how she was able to use her employee discount to buy toys for her children.

She remembered buying a toy oven for Carla.

"It had a little stove and a little sink and you put the water in the back in a container. Then you'd turn on the faucet and the water really came out of the faucet. And then it was an iron, you know, it didn't get hot, just warm enough where they wouldn't burn themselves. Carla loved that! She would say, 'Mommy, help me bake a cake.' So, it baked little cakes and cookies and they loved that."

We all smiled.

I told my mother that Carla had raved about that toy oven for years; and how she would always tell the story of how it was a gift from her mother, listing each and every function it would perform.

Arica asked my mother what is her favorite thing to do currently. I do not think she understood Arica's question.

She answered, "Well, I haven't been around them in a while. It's a long story. But, I'm trying to get things together where I can see my family again."

"We would love it if you came to Kansas City, but we also know that you have a home here and you are used to being here and you're probably comfortable here. It's like, it's kind of scary. I wouldn't want to move to another state. So, like why would you want to?"

"Right. It's a nice place to live for now. You never know what's going to happen when you look ahead, you know. Right now, you know, I'd rather stay here, you know."

Those were her exact words.

Hearing her say this solidified my understanding of the fact that she would prefer to stay where she is for now. However, this was a great opportunity for me to pull out the assisted living information.

Chapter 8
DAY TWO OF OUR VISIT – TALK ABOUT MOVING

"Well, I *did* bring you some information, because Terrance and I would like for you to have it. I had intended on giving it to you yesterday, before you made it clear that you would really like to stay here. But when I told Terrance about it last night, he insisted I give you the information so you could have it. We realize it's your decision to make, but we at least want you to take a look, to know exactly what opportunities lie ahead in case you change your mind."

"Yeah. You never know what's up ahead," she agreed as I pulled out the folder.

I showed her the information for the one assisted living facility in Kansas City I had narrowed down for her. I told her it was just like where she currently lives except she would have her own room. I continued, "You would not have to live with anybody and you can leave your belongings in your room because it would be safe. You would not have to carry anything around for fear of it being stolen. It is a safe place, with twenty-four-hour security, where you could come and go as you please just like you do here." I told her that some of the benefits were weekly housekeeping, laundry service, three meals a day, and medication management. "The nurses come to your room to assist you with taking your medication."

Mother seemed a little nervous when I mentioned the medication part. I felt it was because of what Donna had told me about the issues they had with her not taking her pills and hiding them under her mattress.

"All utilities are included except phone. However, we would provide a phone if you wanted one. This place would empty your trash and provide transportation if you need to run errands. They provide many activities and take the residents on outings, like ball games. They even have a chapel for religious services, and a beauty shop on the campus."

Mother asked, "They have a hairdresser right there?"

"Yes, and if you didn't have the money, *we* would pay for it. We would make sure you had whatever you wanted.

"The room is not furnished so we would have to go and pick out a nice bedroom set, with a comfortable mattress, and a television. You would have a private bathroom with a walk-in shower. The doctor, dentist, podiatrist, and psychiatrist are on site regularly. You would be able to get treatment and rehabilitation for your hip without having to leave the facility. They provide behavioral health as well as assistance with bathing and grooming for those who need it."

Just then, a man walked out of the center room and through the lobby, where we were sitting. He looked over at us.

Mother jokingly said to him, "What are you being nosy over here for? What are you looking for?"

When the man was out of sight, I continued, "This particular place has a couple of rooms open at this time. However, if you decide to move a year or two down the road, we would have to check and see if they have a room available at that time."

Mother said, "Right."

I jokingly said to her, "If you wanted to go home with us now, then they would have a spot for you today."

We all laughed.

Every once in a while, as I was talking about the facility, Mother would say, "Right." This made me feel like she was listening with interest and that she was okay with me continuing to tell her more.

I felt like I had said enough, but I wished I had some pictures of the facility to show her. Arica found some pictures of it on her cell phone and showed them to her. As we looked at the pictures,

Arica and I pointed out the beautiful dining area, the bedroom, and the private bathroom.

She said, "Wow! That's nice, real nice. Oh, boy! I haven't made up my mind yet."

"I want to go ahead and leave this information with you so you can take all the time you need to look at it and think about it.

She reiterated, "That looks like luxury! I'm not ready for anything like that yet. But, I'll give thought to it."

As we were finishing our assisted living discussion, I told her, "It would be nice if you lived in Kansas City because we are not always able to travel here to visit you."

I assured her, "If you were to move, you would still be in control of your own independence. We would not control your life. We would only be there for what *you* wanted us to be there for."

This portion of our visit ended with her saying, "I'll keep it in mind."

Then we moved on to talk about other things.

I told Mother that Terrance, Grayson, and Devon wanted to do a video call with her while Arica and I were there with her. I told her we had planned to do it Saturday if that was okay with her. She said it was okay and said four o'clock would be the best time for her.

I reminded her that Arica and I were taking her out to eat at one o'clock on Sunday. She had forgotten but she said she had wanted to go to Applebee's for a long time. After a revelation such as this it was no brainer where we would be dining on Sunday.

I asked her if there was anything she needed that we could bring to her while we were in town. She said, "Do you really want me to tell you? Money!"

We all laughed.

I told her we would give her some money before we left to go home. At that point, I realized that money was the best thing we could provide to her.

Finding Mother: A Journey of Loss and Love

The Center Counselor, Rashad, came out into the lobby at around two o'clock and asked me if I would go into the hallway to chat with him. The center was to close at three o'clock, so he wanted to have time to chat with me before then.

I asked Mother if it was okay for him to talk to me.

She said, "Yes."

He and I entered the hallway. He expressed that he was very happy to know Geneva had family who cared about her. He had a puzzled look on his face as he revealed to me that Geneva had never mentioned having children. He conducts group sessions with the residents, and she would often shy away from group discussions about family.

I had already heard April and Donna say she never mentioned having children in the many years that they had been working with her. However, when he said it, I felt a sting in my emotions.

How could my mother have lived in denial about having children for so many years? This caused me to open up and begin to talk. Rashad showed great care and concern as he listened to my finding mother story.

As I recounted my side of events, he remained silent, observing me and nodding on occasion to let me know he was paying attention. I told him details about how she left, how I searched and how we recently reunited. I expressed how I had longed to find her and take care of her. I let him know that my ultimate purpose for being there was to woo her into moving closer to us so I could provide for her the way I had always wanted to.

He told me how amazing my story was and asked me a few questions, like, "So, is your father still alive?" and other similar questions. Then he began to tell me the true purpose of asking me to join him in the hallway.

He asked me if I would sign a release form so that he could be free to speak with me anytime concerning my mother's status at the center. I felt pressured even though I knew that was not his intention. He was just performing the part of his job that required him to obtain social history for Geneva, and to build a relationship with her family members. The pressure came from knowing I was not the average family member.

I explained that I was not sure if I wanted to take long-distance responsibility for her so soon after meeting her. I explained that it had been almost fifty years since I had seen her last and that I do not really know her. I felt afraid to commit to any responsibility I would have to take from so many miles away. I told him I had been talking with her about moving to Kansas City to be closer to us so, in which case I would be very comfortable taking full responsibility for her. However, it would be difficult to take care of her when we are in two different states.

I expressed that if she does not even want to be close to us, then why should I commit to taking any responsibility for her?

What he was asking me to do caused me to experience a lot of turmoil, stress and feelings of guilt the whole time we were talking. The thought of receiving a long-distance phone call, that my mother needed help, terrified me. I knew I would be limited to how much I could do because of the distance between us.

Would I sacrifice time and resources to go to her?

Probably not, because I felt like she left years ago because she did not want to be with us. Now she is refusing to live closer to us. So, why should I feel obligated at this stage of our lives?

Sure, I was enjoying her company during our visit, but that did not mean I wanted this type of responsibility for her, at least not long-distance. I told him I would take the form with me, share it with my brothers and give it some thought. He said that would be okay and gave me his card, which included his cell phone number. He invited me to call him anytime.

He confirmed that my mother had a mental illness and he told me her diagnosis. I am purposely not sharing the name of her diagnosis. However, the most common symptoms are delusions, hallucinations, disorganized thinking, abnormal behavior, and not able to function normally. Patients do not necessarily display all the symptoms all of the time. Symptoms range from remission to very severe.

As I considered what the counselor was telling me about my mother's mental illness, I was able to recall observing some of these symptoms in my mother.

During this moment with the counselor, I also thought back about the times when Ashley and Donna had told me about her occasional resistance to take her medication. I thought about how April and Donna told me that as long as she takes it, she is nice and does not bother anybody. However, if she refuses to take it, her uncontrollable behavior places her at risk of being committed, against her will, to a mental hospital.

The counselor went on to explain that one of the main goals of the center was to reunify residents with their family, if possible. He felt like it would be in her best interest to live near her children who loved her and wanted to take good care of her. He encouraged me to stay in touch with her, and said that he would do everything he could to encourage her to make an educated decision to come live with us in Kansas City. In the meantime, he would use group sessions to learn more about her desires and let me know her wants and needs so I could provide some things for her.

On the happy side, he told me she had an interest in knitting. On the unhappy side, he informed me she had been robbed and was afraid of it happening again. He revealed that was how her stuff, that she was telling Arica and I about, got "misplaced."

I paused to think about how a robber had taken her state identification, social security card, birth certificate, and all of her children's information.

This was very hurtful to hear.

I was distressed to know this horrific thing had happened to my own mother. I know it was impossible for me to have been able to protect her from that, but it did not stop me from wishing I could have.

Finding Mother: A Journey of Loss and Love

We ended our conversation with him telling me to think about signing the release and to let him know what I decide to do. It was about fifteen minutes before the center would be closing when I returned to the lobby.

While I was in the hallway talking with the counselor, Arica and Mother had remained in the lobby and continued to talk. When I entered, Arica was asking her one question after another, her face flushed with anticipation of what each answer would be.

"How did you find out your adoptive mother was not your real mother?

"Did you ever want to meet your real mom?"

"What can I call you, Grandmother, Nanny, Nana?"

"What was it like when you first met my mom and her brothers? Were you surprised?

"What is your favorite childhood memory?"

I sat down and listened with much interest as Mother happily answered every one of Arica's questions. The smile and proud look on my mother's face let me know she was enjoying her talk with Arica.

In response to the questions, she said she was sixteen years old when she found out she was adopted, but she did not care because she was used to living with the woman who she called Mother. She said she had the opportunity to meet her biological mother. As far as what name Arica could call her, she said she would prefer for Arica to "just make it simple" and call her Geneva.

I felt a bit sad for my daughter because I believed she expected to be able to use some sort of endearment term to refer to her newly found grandmother. Arica later said she was okay with it and that she did not care.

"I don't really see her as my grandmother anyway," she said.

However, I still felt gloomy because I knew she was missing the experience of having a "normal" grandmother-granddaughter relationship with my mother.

Finding Mother: A Journey of Loss and Love

I felt surprised, yet grateful when Arica asked the question about how Mother felt when she met us. That is something I would never have had the courage to ask. Mother admitted she was surprised and shocked when we showed up.

"I didn't know really what to say when they first came there. Because I don't usually have company. I never had real company, so I didn't know *what* to say!" she said.

I was very interested in what she had to say about meeting us for the first time.

Finally, she shared her favorite childhood memory.

She told Arica and me, "Mother and Father bought me a bike. I would see other kids riding their bikes on this hill and I wished I could ride a bike. So, I saw this bike in this yard. I said, 'I'm going to learn how to ride a bike.' So, I picked it up and went up the hill with the other kids. I went up and down, up and down, until I finally learned how to balance the bike. I was so happy I didn't know what to do! I was telling my girlfriend and some other kids, 'I learned how to ride a bike!'"

She continued, "My mother had told me to stay off bikes. She would say, 'You might fall and hurt yourself.' I *did* fall and the bike didn't even have brakes on it! I took a chance trying to learn, and skinned my knee. But, I said I don't care, I know how to ride a bike now!"

We all laughed.

She continued her story, "All of a sudden, I got afraid. I said, 'Oh my God!' My mother is gonna know that I was on the bike. My knee was skinned up. I said, 'I don't care, I know how to ride a bike!' So, when I got home, I was trying to hide it.

"Mother said, 'How did you get that scar?'

"I said, 'Oh, I just fell.'

"I didn't tell her about the bike.

"She put some peroxide on it to clean it. She felt sorry for me so she didn't spank me that time.

Finding Mother: A Journey of Loss and Love

"So about two weeks after that, Mother and Father surprised me with a new bike!

"I said, 'That's all mine?'

"We had a large back yard. My mother wanted me to ride it in the back yard.

"I said, 'You don't ride bikes in the back yard.'

"I wanted to ride on the street. The other kids rode *theirs* on the street. Little by little, I eased up and started riding on the sidewalk. Then, little by little, I eased to the street. My mother put a bell and a basket on it. So, if I had to go to the store for her, she let me ride the bike."

When my mother finished telling us her new bike story, she explained that she had to ease from the backyard to the street when she got her first pair of skates, too. Before she got her own pair, she had found an abandoned pair on the sidewalk and put them on.

Her mother asked her where she got them.

She answered, "From the sidewalk. Nobody wants them or they wouldn't have left them out here."

Her mother made her put them back.

Soon after, she received her first pair of new skates.

Three o'clock came and our visit ended with all of us laughing about my mother's skate story.

As we were preparing to walk out, I felt proud of Arica for asking so many questions that I would not have thought to ask. I felt elated that my mother was feeling comfortable enough to provide responses.

We walked with mother as she carried her backpack to the elevator to get on the bus heading back to the boarding home. As mother was getting on the elevator, we told her we would be coming to visit her later that evening.

We went back to our hotel, ate a late lunch and got some rest. By then, it was time for us to go visit Mother. Nothing notable happened during that visit. We just sat in the living room, engaged in small talk and looked at the movie that was on the television. We also looked at some more pictures. After a nice and relaxing visit, Arica and I went out for dinner, returned to our hotel and retired to our rooms for the night.

As I lay my head on my pillow to rest for the night, I swirled in my mind what that day had brought about? I learned the true purpose of the center. That it was not merely a place for fun activities, but behavior therapy. We had the wonderful opportunity to talk to my mother, laugh with her, ask her many questions, and listen as she shared loving memories from her childhood. I got the chance to tell her all about the Kansas City assisted living facility I had in mind for her.

Most of all, one of my goals for the trip was fulfilled.

I finally found out how my mother truly felt about moving to Kansas City. I was finally able to stop worrying and relax, accepting that she is okay where she is for now. Like she said, "You never know what the future may hold."

Chapter 9
DAY THREE OF OUR VISIT - SATURDAY

I felt good on Friday, like half of my mission had been accomplished. However, there was still another goal to fulfill. I was not worried because I knew Mother and I would be talking Sunday, so Saturday was just a day to relax and enjoy our time together in the city, before going back to visit her. Arica and I sat outside in the city's downtown area and ate lunch that afternoon.

When we arrived at the boarding home that evening, Mother and the other residents were still sitting in the dining room area eating dinner. She did not see us walk in. We went into the dining room, walked over to two empty chairs at one of the tables and sat down. When she finally saw us, she looked a little puzzled to realize we had been sitting there without her being aware we were there. It was not clear to me exactly why she seemed puzzled.

After a couple of minutes, she asked us to go sit in the living room and wait for her. We sat in there and talked, while also glancing up at the television every once in a while. We waited for her for so long that we began to wonder where she was and what she was doing. We knew she had probably long since finished eating her dinner. Before we arrived, I remembered that my brothers would be waiting for me to call them for a video call with Mother. The time came and she had not come into the living room yet, so I actually forgot about the video call.

After waiting for about fifteen more minutes, I was still wondering why mother was taking so long to join us. I left out of the living room to see where she was and what she was doing. One of the residents noticed I was looking for her and told me she was outside smoking. I went back and sat down on the couch until another fifteen minutes went by.

Finding Mother: A Journey of Loss and Love

Finally, I made my way outside so I could see exactly what she was doing for myself. I found her sitting on the front steps of the boarding home, with her backpack sitting beside her, slowly savoring a cigarette. I figured that was her regular routine when we were not there. I presumed she needed that moment to herself before coming in to hang out with us.

When she saw me come outside, she told me she had given a young man some money and sent him to the store to buy Arica and me some bottles of soda pop. She said she would be in just as soon as he returned. I felt impressed that she thought of the idea to buy us something to drink. We were not big soda pop drinkers, but I did not tell Mother because I felt grateful that she thought of us in that way. I thought that was a very nice thing for her to do.

I went back into the house, strolled back into the living room and sat back down on the couch.

After a while, Mother finally entered the living room with a big smile on her face. Her backpack was in one hand, and two bottles of soda pop was in the other. She held the necks of the bottles in between her fingers. The proud look on her face indicated that she was confident we would be happy about getting the drinks; and that we would feel it was worth the wait to quench our thirst at last.

She gave us our drinks, set her backpack down and sat in between us on the couch.

Suddenly I remembered the video call!

First, I made a video call to Terrance and Grayson. They had agreed to wait together over Grayson's house, since Terrance's phone did not have video call option. When they did not answer the call, I tried several more times. By this time, I was feeling very disappointed with myself for forgetting, and I was feeling bad for having kept them waiting.

They never did answer, so I called Jerome, who answered immediately. He and his wife came face-to-face with Mother and enjoyed a wonderful video call.

Finding Mother: A Journey of Loss and Love

After that, I made a regular voice call to Terrance and found out he had already left Grayson's house. They had waited for my call for an hour, then gave up. I told him how sorry I was and that if he went back around to Grayson's house, I would call again. He assured me it was okay and said he did not have time to go back over.

I take pride in being a person who keeps my word.

Knowing my brothers were waiting and I did not call, made me feel awful. I got over it for the moment, and showed Mother some more of the family photos I had brought. We looked at photos, while glancing up at the television every now and then.

I looked over and noticed Arica had not opened her soda pop. I realized she was not going to drink it because she does not drink pop. I am the same, but I drank it for two reasons: I actually like the flavor that she bought and could not resist, and I truly appreciated her kind gesture.

While my mother was engrossed with turning pages in my picture album, I looked at her and noticed some similarities. I had always wondered why my legs, toes and forehead looked the way they do. They look similar to hers, except her features were more pronounced than mine.

All of a sudden, I heard someone shout, "Medication!" It was a worker in the office. This was a call for all residents to come over to the office door, stand in line and take their medication. Mother continued to look at photos until Arica and I asked her if she needed to take her medication.

She said she would take it later.

Just then, I remembered the story Donna told me about my mother hiding medication under her mattress and not taking it.

I said, "You better go take your medication."
She looked at me with an understanding look on her face, got up off the couch, walked over to the office door, stood in line and took her pill. As she was walking back towards us, I noticed she walked on her tiptoes and did not pick her feet up all the way when she walked.

Finding Mother: A Journey of Loss and Love

It reminded me of the way my father would often scold me. He would say, "Stop walking on your tip toes!" and "Pick your feet up when you walk!"

I also noticed my sense of humor was similar to hers. She understood all of my jokes and I understood hers. We laughed at each other's witticisms. Realizing where I got some of my features and characteristics from caused me to appreciate myself more.

It was getting late and we needed to be getting back to the hotel. As we were wrapping up our visit, and putting away pictures, I reminded Mother we would be taking her out to dinner the next day.

She mentioned that she would be embarrassed about "hopping" into the restaurant due to her hip pain. However, she said she would go and told us to pick her up at one o'clock on Sunday. Hearing her comment about "hopping" into the restaurant made me think she was feeling hesitant about going out to eat with us. However, since she said she would go, I did not push the issue.

I hoped she would keep her promise to go with us. If I managed to take her out, it would be a thing to remember, not to mention that I truly needed to have *that* talk with her about why she left our family.

Arica and I said our goodbyes to Mother, then, we went to a restaurant to have dinner before going back to our hotel. Back at the hotel, I called Terrance again just to make sure he was not upset with me for forgetting to make the video call. Again, he told me it was okay. I offered to put them on a video call when we went back the next day. He told me not to worry about it and that he was fine with not having the call. From that conversation, I felt assured that he did not have any ill feelings about the situation.

I went to bed that night eagerly anticipating the next day, when I would finally have the talk with my mother that I had been waiting for.

Chapter 10
DAY FOUR OF OUR VISIT - SUNDAY

On Sunday morning, I woke up feeling very excited as I looked forward to taking my mother out to dinner and hearing her side of the story of why she left us forty-nine years ago. She had already promised we could discuss it. So, I was bursting with joy over what this day would bring. I was planning on striking up the conversation when we took her out for dinner. There we would have privacy away from the boarding home, in which people were always around.

For months, ever since our reunion visit, I had been looking forward to my mother talking to me about why she left.

I was not able to ask about it during the initial reunion visit because I felt like it was too soon since we had just met her again after so many years. It had taken a long time for her to finally open up to us during that visit. When she did, she only talked about positive things that made her smile. I sensed strongly that she would not feel comfortable opening up about why she left. So, I refrained from asking her about it at that time.

However, after my brothers and I had returned home from our initial reunion visit, I was talking to her on the phone. I had asked her if she would be okay with talking to me about why she left. She told me she would be okay with it, but she could not talk about it over the phone because office workers were listening and she did not want them to know her business. I was happy to learn that she was willing to talk about it. So, for months, I had looked forward to the precise moment in time that I would be sitting next to her listening as she openly shared her story.

After rising out of bed, Arica and I packed our suitcases, put them in the car and checked out of the hotel. We skipped breakfast in our anticipation of taking mother out to eat. Since she was expecting us to come at one o'clock, we had the entire morning to do whatever we wanted to do.

We went shopping.

I had observed that the flip-flop shoes she was wearing did not provide the support I felt she needed for her feet. So, I bought her some comfortable sandals and some socks before going over.

It was around noon when we finished shopping.

Having nothing else to do, we went on over to the boarding home. When we got there, we exited our vehicle and walked to the front of the boarding home. Geneva was sitting outside on the front steps smoking a cigarette.

"You all are early," she said.

I couldn't help but marvel at the way she was cognizant about the time of day. I had been carrying an incorrect assumption that she was not supposed to know what month, day or time it was due to her mental illness. As always, she was acutely aware.

We explained that we did not have anything else to do after shopping, so we just came on over.

Just then, she announced, "I'm not going!"

My excitement evaporated immediately at her words. That was a moment I had looked forward to for months. The moment that I would finally be able to spend time with her away from the boarding home and get the answers I needed about why she left our family.

In an instant, I remembered the evening before, when she talked about her reluctance to go out to eat with us. I recalled in my mind how she had mentioned feeling embarrassed about the idea of "hopping" into a restaurant due to her painful hip.

Even though I felt disappointed about her backing out, I understood where she was coming from. I could not be angry with her for deciding not to go. She had given us fair warning that she may be uncomfortable about going out in public. I just did not take full heed to her warning due to being so enthusiastic about the possibility of it all.

Finding Mother: A Journey of Loss and Love

It quickly dawned on me that she was accustomed to being either at the boarding home or at the center. She had not been acclimated into going out to public places. So, although she said yes at first, I believe she changed her mind when she realized it would not be realistic for her to "limp" herself into a public place after being sheltered in mental health facilities for so many years.

After getting over the initial shock of her proclamation that she was not going, I noticed a lady sitting on the front steps smoking with my mother. She was a resident of the boarding home.

She introduced herself and asked who we were.

Geneva offered her usual answer of how it was none of her business who we were.

At the same time, I was saying, "This is *my* daughter," pointing at Arica, and "I am *her* daughter!" pointing at Geneva.

The woman said, "Geneva, I didn't know you had children!"

Geneva just stared ahead with a blank look on her face and did not respond. She did not seem upset about me telling her secret, however.

I realized she had lived in denial about having children for so many years and that she did not like people knowing her business. However, I got the feeling that she was okay with me telling the truth and that she would not dare want to risk crushing me by denying me to the woman after I had claimed her with so much excitement.

I wondered if she had been in denial as a way of burying the emotional pain and embarrassment of having left us so many years ago. Everyone who I met at the boarding home acted shocked about Geneva having children. Some of them had known her for over fifteen years, and they never had a clue she had given birth.

After a few moments, I accepted the fact that my mother was not going to allow us to take her out to eat.

In my heart, I still needed to hear her tell me her story of why she left.

Finding Mother: A Journey of Loss and Love

I felt determined not to leave town without having that conversation with her. I offered to spend some time with her there at the boarding home before we got on the road back to Kansas City. She accepted my offer and seemed happy about having us stay and visit with her for a while. I told her I bought her some sandals and socks and that I was going to give them to her when we went out to eat. Since we were not going, I asked her if I could go get the items out of the car and give them to her.

She said that would be okay.

I went to the car and came back to the front of the house with the shopping bag in my hand. I took out the items and showed them to her. She tried on the shoes and said they were very comfortable. She really liked them a lot.

After she had finished smoking, she stood up and picked up her backpack. Then she invited us inside and asked, "Do you want to sit where we were sitting yesterday?" She was referring to the living room, where other residents were sitting and the television was up very loud, making it hard to hear each other talk.

This was my absolute last opportunity to talk to her about why she left and I knew it would be difficult, if not impossible to talk about it in the living room.

So, I responded, "No."

She said it was more comfortable in there.

I said, "It is? Oh okay."

We all went into the living room. Arica and I sat down on the couch. My mother announced she would be right back and left out of the room, leaving her backpack on the floor in front of the couch.

While she was gone, I expressed to Arica that I wished the television was not on. I was afraid it would interfere with my mission of talking with my mother about why she left. Not only was the television on, but once again it was very loud. I thought even if we were able to talk, we might not be able to hear each other.

We could not just turn it down because for one, it was mounted high up on the wall, not to mention that other people were watching it, *and* we were just the visitors with no say on the matter.

We chatted until finally my mother walked back in. She was wearing the comfortable sandals I had just given her.

I asked, "How do those feel?"

"Nice and comfy," she said, just before sitting down in between Arica and me on the couch. I did not bring any pictures for her to look at this time.

Mother asked us where we stayed, and we told her the name of the hotel. She had never heard of that hotel. She began to tell us about various other hotels that she knew about in the area.

As she was talking, I remembered how well Arica was able to inspire her to open up and talk on Friday. So, I asked Arica if she had any "questions." We both laughed because she knew exactly what I meant: the type of questions that would help my mother open up and give me the answers I so desperately needed from her. We were at the end of our visit and I wanted to hear her tell me her story of why she left. Arica did not have any questions at that time, but Mother did.

"Did you hear from Terrance?" she asked.

She was referring to the situation the day before when I failed to call Terrance and Grayson on time for the four o'clock video call as I had promised. I told her I had talked to him and he had forgiven me.

Chapter 11
DAY FOUR OF OUR VISIT – WHY MOTHER LEFT

Suddenly, mother started laughing about something on television. Feeling tensed, I was nervously trying to find a way to ask my mother about why she left.

Feeling afraid of her rejecting my inquiry, I began by saying, "So, you'll never tell me? I really want to know. You don't think you'll ever share?"

Somehow, she understood exactly what I was trying to say.

She responded, "I'm a private person."

Desperately trying to appease her with hopes she would open up and begin to give me the answers I needed, I replied, "I'm the same way. In fact, a lot of your children are the same way."

"Are they?" she said.

Still feeling extremely petrified I rambled, "So, I totally understand that. Yeah. But, I mean like I just really want to hear from you. You know. Because I've heard a lot of stuff. But, I just want to hear from you."

She said, "Right."

I continued, "I feel like I know. I just want to hear you say the actual words."

Mother had a nervous look on her face as she pointed at the woman who was working in the office.

"Can she hear us?" I asked.

She replied, "When we be on the phone, she eavesdrops and then she will gossip. So, I don't want to come right out with anything. You know?"

By now, I was feeling extremely discouraged.

I responded timidly, "Oh okay. That's why I thought we could talk since I'm here, and I don't know when I'll be back again.

Finding Mother: A Journey of Loss and Love

The next time I talk to you, it will probably be on the phone, and I *know* you will not be able to talk then. While I'm here, like this is like the perfect time. And if you can't talk now, then I guess, it's kind of like a now or never situation."

Mother laughed, "Now or never."

Unsure of what was funny, I told her, "That is how I feel."

She said, "That's the name of a song."

I responded, "Yep. Maybe we can go outside and talk."

Mother totally disregarded my request to go outside.

Looking up at the television, she asked, "That's the movie we saw last night, isn't it?"

"Yes, that's the same one," I said.

By that time, it appeared I would be going back to Kansas City without my concerns being satisfied. I knew once we left, I would never ever get the answers I needed so badly. I was feeling sad and disheartened, yet frustrated. The thought of leaving without hearing her story devastated me.

One of my two desires for returning had been met, but it seemed I would carry the other one for the rest of my life. As I basked in my feelings of desolation, my mother made a humorous comment about a commercial that came on television.

Feeling hugely embarrassed about what was happening, I looked over at Arica, who had been quiet the whole time, and saw her eyes were teary.

Finally, she said something.

"Miss Geneva," she said. "I know I don't know when we are going to see you again. I respect your decision not to share. I want you to know that there are a lot of us that have questions about our past. You know? Who we are, where we came from…"

"Right," said Mother.

Arica continued, "…Why we are the way we are. I know that some of the things my mom has been told has been hurtful to her. She's been told that you didn't want her. But, we don't know. You know it's like we just have questions…"

Finding Mother: A Journey of Loss and Love

"Yeah," Mother agreed.

Arica continued, "If there was anything that you *did* feel comfortable sharing, could you share *something* that you do feel comfortable with? Just *anything* that is true so that we can fill in some holes, fill in some gaps..."

It was obvious to me that Arica's plea genuinely touched my mother's emotions and caused her to understand how important it was for her to open up and share her story.

It was at that point that I think my mother realized we had no intentions of leaving without the answers I needed.

Seeing the change in my mother's countenance caused me to feel so very grateful that Arica was there with me. She knew exactly the right words to say and how to articulate them in a way that pricked my mother's heart.

"Right. Well uh," Mother said.

Seeing she was ready to speak freely, I said, "We can go somewhere where it is quiet if you want."

Mother reverted, "Are you sure my husband is dead?" She was referring to my father.

I was feeling like, even though my mother was prepared to share, she was afraid to begin for fear my father could be still alive, for fear he would be upset with her for telling me her side of the story.

In response to her concern I said, "Yes. I am sure he has passed away." I stopped for a moment, trying to contain my emotions. "He and grandmother told me you left and you did not want me. But, even if that was the case, I forgive you."

Mother laughed a grateful laugh, as if she was relieved to hear me say that.

I continued, "But, I just want to hear the story from you, that's all."

Mother took a deep breath as if she tried to brace herself for what she was about to reveal.

Finding Mother: A Journey of Loss and Love

"It all began before you were born. I would often feel tired from taking care of the five kids your father and I had together. He would go out of town for work, leaving me alone with them for one or two weeks at a time. I told him I needed a break from the kids…"

Clearly, it was hard for her to delve into her emotions and relive all of those unpleasant memories, but she was doing it for me.

From her story, coupled with things I already knew, I gathered that she had already been in and out of mental facilities several times before I was even born. I had concluded that she was a patient in a mental hospital at the time of my birth, and that my father had taken me home from the hospital. If he had not, the State of Michigan would have taken custody of me and would have likely gotten adopted – just like the additional four children she had after she left us. Somehow, between her hospital stays, our family ended up in Kansas City, where she experienced her final mental hospital stay before leaving our family for good.

Her story was somewhat choppy, so I had to piece things together. Nevertheless, I felt happy and relieved that she was finally opening up.

This was the moment I had been waiting to have with my mother.

I was basking in it as I listened intently to every word she had to say, even if the story was rather difficult to follow.

She continued, "My husband and my mother arranged to have me put in a hospital. They told me it was a regular hospital, that would help my body rejuvenate and give me some rest from the kids. After I was admitted, I found out it was a mental hospital. Your father thought it was just a normal hospital. He didn't know it was a mental hospital, you know."

Hearing her say this, I felt reasonably sure he knew but he and my grandmother just had to trick her into going because she may not have cooperated otherwise. I also felt reasonably sure that she was likely suffering from the symptoms of her mental illness during that time, and that was why they tricked her in that manner.

Finding Mother: A Journey of Loss and Love

She went on, "I had a good up-bringing and a good relationship with my mother and my husband. They didn't really talk to me about personal stuff. They kept it to themselves. I really didn't know much, either, around that time. He didn't talk to me that much.

"He was nice to me. He just wanted me to feel better."

She recalled being in the mental hospital and no one ever coming to see her.

"He stayed away. My mother came only one time and she brought Danisha with her, and that was it. I was in that place for two years with no visitors."

Hearing that part of her story, I tried to put two-and-two together.

I thought, "She is saying she was in a mental facility for two years, with no visitors, just before she left. However, I was two years old when she left, and I have several specific memories of her being at home during the two years that she was claiming to have been locked away with no visitors."

I told her, "I specifically remember you being at home."

"I would come home on furlough." She said.

Hearing this part of her story brought back a vague memory that I had been carrying. I was a toddler, and my grandmother had driven me to the hospital where my mother was a patient. Anxious to see her, I was heartbroken when we arrived and I was not allowed to go into the area where her room was. Memories of why were not clear, but my devastation was vivid.

I realized that Mother was doing her very best to share only the things she was comfortable sharing. I also realized she could possibly be confused about the order in which some of the events took place so long ago.

I tried to refrain from thinking she would be purposely lying to me. Even if she was, I would still be understanding towards her because she has every reason to experience feelings of shame about the details of her past life.

Finding Mother: A Journey of Loss and Love

She alleged, "There is a lot I don't know. I did not have a chance to talk to my husband before I left the mental hospital with my friend. He said he had family in another town so that is where we went."

As she was telling me that part of her story, I was thinking about how my father and grandmother told me she had professed, "I'm in love with Calvin," just before she ran away from the mental hospital.

"Did you at least say goodbye to Grandmother before you left?" I asked.

"Yes, I told her bye-bye."

She said a few more things, then, ended that part of her story by saying, "And that's all I know."

Although some of her story did not add up or match what I had always believed, I was still very appreciative that she had shared it with me. I told her I understood everything she had just expressed.

I mentioned that I remember my father hitting her a lot.

"Do you remember that?" I asked her.

"One time, we were on our way to church. Your father hit *at* me. He was angry about something, but never explained it to me. He just hit me, you know? And that's all it was."

I told her, "I remember him hitting you, and it was not right. I don't care what your mental state was, you did not deserve to be hit, ever."

She started talking about the people upstairs on the "third floor" again.

From my time with my mother, she usually starts reverting to the "third floor" to avoid dealing with the reality of painful memories. I believe the "people upstairs" were actually voices she was hearing in her head. However, she did not perceive the voices as being in her head. She believed they were in the same house with her, but on a different floor in the boarding home.

I was hoping she still had more to tell me about her story.

Finding Mother: A Journey of Loss and Love

On the other hand, I was hoping she was feeling at peace about having opened up about things she had been keeping to herself for so many years.

I assured her, "You can tell me anything. There is not anything you could that would surprise me.

"I feel like I pretty much know the details surrounding why you left, but I just need to hear it from you."

Again, she reverted to talking about the voices from "upstairs." As an attempt to bring her focus back to our talk, I asked her some questions.

"Do you remember telling my father you were in love with Calvin?"

She said, "No, the people upstairs told him that."

"Do you remember saying you did not want your kids?"

"No, I never said anything like that. I was away from them for a long time. One time, I was in a mental hospital and the staff told me, 'Your family is here.'"

Mother's face displayed a look of distress.

"But, they never told me where you all were, and so I never knew what had happened to my family."

She looked down in sadness.

I was unable to place the exact timeframe of that incident, as she seemed confused about exactly when it had happened.

"Do you ever feel angry with my father for hitting you?"

"Besides the tap on my hand on our way to church, he treated me good. There is nothing for me to be angry about. He was nice to me otherwise, but it could have been something that was going on away from me and he didn't want to tell."

She continued, "We were on our way to church and he just, you know, he just spanked me on my hand like *that*."

She tapped me on my hand to show me how he had hit her.

Her recollection of my father's abuse was very surprising to me because I specifically remember my daddy beating on her. Furthermore, he never denied it. He specifically said he "had to knock some sense into her." It seemed to me she was in denial, and was making light of, and excuses for, my father's actions.

I told her, "I remember standing outside of your and his bedroom and hearing you crying as he was striking you. I would feel heartbroken. You did not deserve that."

She said, "He was nice to me, you know? I taught my children to love their father and they did."

I had spent many years thinking she had left because my father beat her. But, her responses to my questions made me feel like that was not the reason at all. In her mind, he was good to her and she had no reason to be angry with him. This left me with a new question:

"So, do you remember what caused you to leave?" I asked.

She answered in these exact words, "Let's see how did this start? It's been a long time. Oh yeah, we went to…after I was in the hospital for a while, they um sent me on a plane to go to Kansas City where my mother was. And so, after we stayed there for a while, he had a place… a house there and uh, so let's see…all the kids they were happy to see me and we were happy together, you know? Really, they loved me and I loved them. So, um, I was pregnant with you. And so, uh I had to go to the hospital and have you. And um…"

I interjected, "I had ordered my birth records and it looked like my daddy took me home from the hospital. It appeared you did not take me home."

She said, "Right. And I was in the hospital, too. They never talked to me about anything."

"Were you in a mental hospital at the time of my birth?" She said, "Yes."

I told her, "I thought maybe that was the case, and maybe that was why you were not able to take me home."

She mentioned the people "upstairs" again. Then she mumbled something about my father still having their marriage license. It seemed like she was saying she was not sure if she and my father were divorced.

"Do you think you and my father are still married?"

She said, "Yes."

"After you left, the court granted him a divorce without you since you were not there anymore."

Most of the questions I asked her were based on negative memories and experiences, and I expected her to tell me she left because she was being beaten or that she was hurting, or perhaps because she was angry with my father or my grandmother.

But, none of those were the case.

She told me, "I didn't really know too much about the negative side because I was not around to know about it. All I knew was the positive side of the life I had with my family."

She admitted she left with Calvin because my father never came when she was in the mental hospital.

"Did you and Calvin get married?"

She said, "Yes," and told me the state where they were married, which explained why I was never able to find a marriage license for the two of them in the states where I was searching. I had no clue that Mother had ever been in the state where they actually got married. So, I had never searched there.

By now, it was clear that I had finally fulfilled my mission of hearing my mother tell me her story of why she left.

For so long, I felt like my mother had abandoned her family. However, after listening to her side of the story, it seems her family may have abandoned her long before she ever left. I have been feeling rejected for all of those years and it seems she may have, in a sense, been feeling rejected, too.

Chapter 12
DAY FOUR OF OUR VISIT – RETURNING HOME

Arica sat patiently the whole time my mother and I were talking. Then she asked, "Are you doing okay?"

Mother said, "Yes, I'm okay."

With the stress of our conversation being over, Mother invited us to move from the living room into the dining room. As we were getting ready to leave the room, Arica offered to carry the backpack for her and she let her. Arica struggled greatly as she was picking it up. Then she looked at my mother as if to wonder how in the world this tiny, delicate looking woman has the strength to carry around such a heavy bag.

"Miss. Geneva, this is heavy! How do you do it?"

My mother replied, "I'm a strong woman, you just don't know!"

We all laughed.

During our entire visit, I had wondered what exactly was in that backpack.

After we had settled in the dining room, Arica thanked my mother for sharing her story.

She said, "You only shared what you were comfortable with right?"

Mother said, "Yes."

Then Arica asked some questions like, "Did you play the piano?" And, "Did you sing, too?"

Mother answered yes to both. Then she began to talk some more about people in the boarding home stealing her clothes and other belongings. "They even stole my Bible! Can you imagine who would want to steal a Bible? They don't read it!"

We all laughed.

Finding Mother: A Journey of Loss and Love

I reminded her that is why I really wished she could move away from there and live closer to us. "I could take you shopping right now, but I know if you bring new things back here, someone would steal it. If you were there with us, you would have your own room, and we could buy you things without having to worry about it getting stolen."

She said, "That sounds good!"

I asked her if she was going be thinking about moving or if she pretty much knows she wants to stay there.

She admitted she likes where she is and that the stealing was not a factor in her decision to stay there. She reiterated that she likes that they have done many things to fix up the boarding home, like painting the walls. She said she likes the convenience of being close to the store, laundry mat, and bus stop.

I told her I understood. While I wish she felt differently, I accepted her reasons for wanting to stay where she was.

She said she was not sure how she had lost all of her children, that details of it were a blur and no one ever explained it to her. She recalled a time when she went back to a house, where children from her second marriage were living, and found the house boarded up.

"I felt devastated. I didn't know what had happened to my kids, or why they had taken them away."

My heart wept for her at that moment.

I told her I had taken some steps to search for them and asked if she knew the names of the hospitals where they were born. She gave me the names of the hospitals. I could not wait to get home and submit this information to Elsie to see if it would help her locate them in her database.

Our visit was rapidly ending. We used my cell phone to take some pictures with Mother. When I showed her one of the pictures on my cell phone screen, she said, "Wow, I am much prettier than I thought I was!"

We all smiled.

Finding Mother: A Journey of Loss and Love

I kept my promise to give her some cash. To show me how much she appreciated the money, she smiled very big, told me "thank you" and gave me a great big kiss on my jaw. We gave our final goodbyes and hugs, then Arica and I walked out of the boarding home, went to the car, hopped in and headed towards the highway to begin our very long drive back to Kansas City.

Arica and I had enjoyed the city. We had partaken in great conversations with my mother, and I knew I had received all the answers I was to going to acquire from her. As we traveled home, I did a lot of thinking about how I felt our visit had gone. I appreciated my mother for doing the best she could to talk to me about why she left.

Even though she was forced to admit herself into a mental hospital around that time, and even though she said there was a lot that she, herself, still did not know surrounding that era, I still felt like there was more she could have shared with me.

I believed she was in denial about a lot of the ways she was feeling back then. I believed she may have been experiencing a lot of guilt for not wanting her children. She did not admit to not wanting us, but I believe it was true.

I valued the things she felt comfortable sharing, but I felt doubtful that she had truly given me all the facts. Therefore, I just had to accept the reality that I may never know her full story.

I wanted her to say she was ready to move, but she did not. The good thing is that I realized my mother's basic needs were being met. I was intrigued to learn that the center is not merely social engagement just to give boarding home residents something fun to do. It is actually a mental health treatment center.

Since she was satisfied to stay where she was, I had to accept the fact that she may never live in Kansas City with us.

Overall, I was impressed with the work of the boarding home and mental health treatment center. I realized they are committed to that specific community of people. They have taken on the challenge of providing their basic physical, emotional and mental health needs. I realized that if it were not for the boarding home and the center, every single person living there would probably be homeless. So, I appreciate the work they are doing and I am grateful they have provided a home for my mother.

Even though I knew exactly how my mother felt about staying where she was for now, I still had a strong desire for her to move closer to us. I did not want any mother of mine to have to carry a heavy backpack around all the time. I imagined her being able to leave her belongings in a room of her own, that she does not have to share. I imagined her having a key to her own room and not having to worry about the other residents coming in and taking her stuff. It was hard for me to wipe out the images in my head of her carrying that big black backpack everywhere she went.

Ultimately, I felt like I got the answers I traveled so many miles for.

I felt grateful that Arica was there with me. I never would have gotten the answers I needed without her. When I took her with me, I did not think about the fact that I was actually taking a licensed social worker with me. I just figured I was taking my daughter for companionship and support. However, having her with me made a world of difference and I cannot begin to imagine how the trip would have gone without her being there.

Due to some things being a blur, Mother was not able to provide clear answers for all of my questions surrounding her departure. However, she gave her sincere responses to my two inquiries. So, I felt like I could not ask for anything more than that.

Nevertheless, a part of me still felt a little disheartened that my two desires remained only partially fulfilled. Therefore, the end of this trip served as time of overall acceptance:

Accepting that Mother actually did not want me, that she left me in the hospital when I was born, and that she left four additional children after she left our family of six children.

Accepting that she left of her own accord, not because of anything my father or grandmother had done.

Accepting that she is mentally ill; that this nice, smart woman is actually sick, and unable to be a mother to me.

Accepting the horrific fact that someone robbed her.

Accepting her poverty-stricken living environment; that she is happy where she is; and that she is not interested in allowing us to provide a better life for her in Kansas City.

Accepting the fact that I may never get her full story without her referring to the people on the "third floor."

I felt I had no choice but to accept all of these things, since this is the way things are and I cannot change it. This left me with a lot of thoughts and feeling as Arica and I were leaving, returning home to Kansas City.

For the next few months after that visit, I experienced an assortment of emotions. I am very transparent about them in the next book from the *Finding Mother Series* entitled, *Diary of Emotions: Thoughts and Feelings*.

Book Four

Diary of Emotions: Thoughts and Feelings

Finding Mother: A Journey of Loss and Love

"When someone in your family has a mental illness, it is easy to say, 'I am going to look past their behavior because I understand that they have a mental illness.'

"Nevertheless, that does not take away the pain that comes with not having the type of relationship that you would like to have with them.

"Sometimes, I wonder what is harder: living without a mother and not knowing her, or knowing her and having to live with the reality of her mental illness."

Grace LaJoy Henderson
Diary of Emotions

DEDICATION

To everyone who has read this book before it was published, when it was only a draft. Your feedback was priceless. Thank you for expressing the value you felt this book might have on the lives of others who may be experiencing similar situations and emotions.

FOREWORD

Nobody likes to "hurry up and wait." However, life events can keep us stagnant. This is the current quandary of the author. This book is appropriately entitled *Diary of Emotions: Thoughts and Feelings*. In this book, the author goes through an up and down, back and forth, tug of war between her heart and her head. She is in a perpetual "She loves me, she loves me not" emotional pattern as she strives to discern her mother's true feelings.

She found her mentally ill mother after 49 years and desires to take care of her. However, she cannot get her mother to move to Kansas City, so that she and her siblings can tend to her needs and improve the quality of her life. It seems her mother is so used to living in a state of poverty, that living in abundance scares her. The author is struggling with the challenges of maintaining this type of long-distance connection.

The entries in this diary reveal that the author is experiencing a very natural stage of the new relationship with her mother. Enough time has not passed for her to be able to accept the reality of who her mother really is. It seems she desires a "typical" mother-daughter relationship, but may never have it due to her mother's condition. This leaves the author feeling impatient and, at times, overwhelmed.

It seems closure is nowhere in sight for the author at this time. Therefore, she continues to go through a very common thought process that many of us go through when a life circumstance disappoints us.

This diary is a very interesting and enjoyable read. It is an excellent window for people to look into the author's heart. It can help readers learn to open windows of their own souls in the midst of challenging life experiences. The book is full of anticipation for the author and her mother to permanently connect in a way that ensures positive outcomes!

~**Phyllis Harris, Former Missouri State Director**
Parent Information Resource Center

FOREWORD

As a school counselor, students come into my office everyday who struggle with emotion management. A significant part of their struggle is that they feel alone as they maneuver through tough times. They think they are the only ones who are confused about how they should feel.

Diary of Emotions: Thoughts and Feelings demonstrates that we all are subject to endure emotional turmoil at some point in our lives. It illustrates that it is okay to be confused or unsure.

Although we believe things will work out in the end, it is necessary that we give ourselves the time and space to feel these emotions no matter how conflicting or difficult they may be.

I definitely believe that this book could benefit secondary school students.

~Jacob Kelow, M.S.Ed.
Secondary School Counselor
Kansas City Public Schools

PREFACE

In *Diary of Emotions,* I delve into the depths of my heart to give you a detailed account about my inner turmoil as well as my mixed feelings about my mother. Having forgiven my mother a long time ago, I strive to make her happy while trying to protect my own heart and soul against the challenge that is a mother suffering from mental illness.

Finding Mother: A Journey of Loss and Love

INTRODUCTION

Hopefully by now, you have read my foster care story and the other three books in the *Finding Mother Series*, all of which have led up to the thoughts and feelings I share in this one.

The thread throughout this book seems to be me toiling with: Should I stop calling my mother? Should I continue sending packages to her? There are sensible reasons to justify stopping both the calls and the packages. However, there are also justifications to continue. So far, I have kept on because a part of me feels like it would be wrong to stop, knowing that she has a mental illness and she may actually need my consistency regardless of how I feel about it.

It is hard to imagine stopping entirely, but I am strongly considering it. The things I have sent lately have either been lost in the mail or stolen by my mother's housemates. That has discouraged me from wanting to send things. Then, couple that with the fact she may not come to the phone, or call me, to confirm whether she received what I have sent. Overall, regardless of what I decide, I will be forever grateful that I found her and that I know where she is.

When I first began journaling, I expressed myself in my audio recorder. Later, I transcribed the audio recordings onto paper. Then, I carefully edited each one. The entries will reveal the way I went back and forth in my thoughts and feelings, as I pondered everything I had learned since finding my mother. In order to keep my true intended tone of voice, this book may feature some improper grammar and sentence structure. Since this is a "diary," I wanted to preserve the way I actually spoke, and not remove it during the editing process.

I believe readers will be interested in my thoughts and feelings because they will be able to understand, relate to, and analyze them. So, travel with me into an array of thoughts and feelings as you read my *Diary of Emotions*.

Finding Mother: A Journey of Loss and Love

AFTER MY SECOND TRIP

When I returned home from the second trip to visit my mother, I kept in close contact with her counselor, Rashad. He and I talked about the release of information form that he had asked me to sign so that he would be able to talk openly with me about my mother. He calmed my concerns by explaining that he did not expect me to take any major responsibility for her.

The form would just allow me to be able to call and learn how she is doing or if she needs anything. I finally decided to sign the paper. However, when I picked up the form to sign it, I realized it was not my signature he needed, but hers. She was the one who needed to grant permission for him to talk to me. I went ahead and signed it per his request, then he also obtained her signature.

Rashad answered his phone whenever I called and he was always available. He listened attentively whenever I spoke. He provided me with great insight about my mother's mental condition.

I appreciated him so much, until finally one day I called him on his cell phone and he informed me he was no longer working for the center. He had been fired because, while he was great when it came to communicating with families, he struggled with some of the other aspects of social work, like documentation of the patient files. I told him how great I thought he was and that I would miss him. He was very knowledgeable about how to interact with families who are going through a crisis. Needless to say, I was saddened to learn of his departure. He was the only one who had actually answered his phone.

Before I met the center staff, I used to call the office numbers, but the phones constantly went unanswered. When I met the center manager, Donna, she told me no one ever answers the office phone and gave me her cell phone number. I felt like I would finally be able to call and actually talk to someone. After going back home to Kansas City, she answered my call twice and then she stopped altogether. Therefore, at this time, I have no one at the mental health treatment center to talk to about my mother's status. The boarding home staff are still available, however.

When I returned home from the second trip, Elsie had not yet given me the results from searching my siblings' names and dates of birth. Therefore, I sent a revised email to her including the new hospital information. With this additional information, I was feeling more and more encouraged that she would be able to locate my siblings in her database.

However, one week later, Elsie finally sent me a response letting me know that her agency did not handle any adoptions for my siblings. She told me that another agency might have handled their adoptions. I felt surprised, yet disappointed, that even with all of the information I had, she was still unable to locate them in her database. However, as she said, another agency may have handled their adoption. For now, I have given up on searching for the four children my mother had after she left.

July 20, 2018

It is weird that my mother can leave me and I can still forgive her. Or have I really forgiven her? That is another issue, I guess. I feel like maybe I have forgiven her. Pretty much for years, I had *totally* forgiven her. I did not blame her for anything. However, now I have met her and it appears she actually did not want us.

Seeing that she does not want to be with us, I feel like I should place some of the blame on her. I know she was not capable of raising us, but even knowing that, it still makes me want to accuse her of something. I feel like, "How does a mother just abandon her children and not want come be with them when they find her?" Well, she has a mental illness and that is how she can do that.

Still it hurts that my mother has mental problems to the point where she does not want her children. Yet she seems so alert, like she understands life.

Her mental illness has been diagnosed so obviously it is real.

Still, I do not know how to feel about her. I sent her some things, and I guess that is all I really want, is just to be able to send her some things when I feel like it. A part of me wants to do things for her all the time, to take care her. It seems she sees me as like a friend I guess; or maybe she sees me as more than a friend. I do not know. It is hard to fathom how a mother could not want to be close to her children. Like if I do not call her, we do not talk. If I stopped calling her, I would never hear from her again, even though she has my phone number. Then again, it may be for the best.

Finding Mother: A Journey of Loss and Love

August 11, 2018

I called my mother today and she did not come to the phone. It has been a few weeks since the last time we talked because I had been feeling like she would rather be to herself. In the past, it seemed like she wanted to say she did not feel like talking, but she never said it. She always came to the phone.

This is the time when I least expected it and this is when it finally happened. I just hope she is ok. Perhaps she has not been taking her medication, and that could be why she did not want to converse with anybody. That would be my only concern, because she always acts like she wants to talk when I call her.

She may just be more comfortable not communicating with anybody since she has been on her own for so long. I have always suspected that, but every time I called, it seemed like she was happy to speak with me, happy that I called, so I did not want to *not* call her and leave her wondering, "Why isn't anybody calling me?" However, if she does not really care to hear from anybody then, I am okay with not calling her.

The last time I called, she came to the phone. She was saying she had to get off the phone for some reason, which was unclear. However, a couple of moments later she said, "I enjoy it when you call." I felt like maybe that might have been her way of saying, "Even though I enjoy these phone calls, I just do not care much for being on the phone." Furthermore, whenever we are on the phone, she says, "Well, yeah, I was sleeping," or "I was in my room getting my clothes ready for the week."

I'll say, "Okay then, I will not keep you."

But, then she'll say, "So, how have you been doing?" kind of like she does not really care to talk but she does not want to hurt my feelings.

I have always sort of felt like maybe she preferred not to be on the phone. I guess she is not going to say how she really feels. She is not going to tell me she does not want to talk to me because we found after almost fifty years.

Finding Mother: A Journey of Loss and Love

Like, how do you tell your daughter, "I really do not need to talk to you?"

It would be okay if she said that to me because it would help me; and that way I would not call because I would understand where she is coming from and how she feels. That way we would have an understanding, as opposed to just acting it out.

I just did not want her to feel like nobody was calling her. I am okay with not calling her considering I do not know her that well and there is not really anything I need from a mother. The only thing I really needed was to hear her tell me why she left in her own words. I needed to know if she wanted to move to Kansas City. I got the answers I desired, so technically there is nothing else I need.

It would be nice if she were a mother who I could talk to about things; if I could tell her what I am going through with my sister, who also has a mental illness, and she could say, "Yeah well this is what worked for me and this is what you could do for her."

I just wish I could talk to her about some things but I know that she is on medication and trying to deal with her own inner emotions, thoughts, and feelings; and trying to keep from cussing people out when they do stuff to her. She is just not capable of doing anything for anyone.

For instance, when Arica and I were visiting with her she said, "That is just somebody else wanting something from me." I do not remember why she made that statement. But, it made me feel like she feels people just want things from her, and I think the bottom line is she is just not able to give anything.

It does feel nice to talk with her when she shares what is on her mind. I do not necessarily need that because I have been without her for so long. Even though I know where she is, I also know she is not able to have the kind of relationship with me that I would want from a mother. I guess a part of me wants to support her in a bigger way, but when I call her and she says she does not feel like talking to anyone, well then, I feel like I should just let her have her life, you know?

Finding Mother: A Journey of Loss and Love

Why should I force anything if she is happy with her life?

I would like to send her *something*, but only on special occasions. Not like a long-standing relationship. Maybe not talk to her every other week or so but, only if it is like Christmas, Mother's Day or her birthday, just to acknowledge her.

It is kind of a cool knowing where she is and knowing that she is okay, finally, after all these years, and having a sincere understanding that she is just not able to be a mother.

I realize there is a lot I still do not know about her. Yet, I feel a sense of responsibility for her just because she gave birth to me. However, she left me in the hospital and my dad had to take me home. That makes me question my sense of responsibility.

However, I do not foresee it vanishing, because I intend to send her some things soon. Maybe some pants, maybe a winter coat. She could probably use some long socks, especially with the winter months coming up; maybe a sweater or two. Maybe a turban to wear on her head. I think she would appreciate it, but I also think she is content, even if I do not send her things.

I do not know whether I should send her a coat. She mentioned wanting to have a coat with some pockets on the inside. However, I know that she has the means to keep warm because it was cold outside when we were there, and she was wearing that leather coat and black hat, and she had on her little tennis shoes. She was warm and her needs were met.

I do not know if she would wear the turban, but you never know. The turban might be too much for her. She might think, "this is too flashy." However, I think she would be okay with some socks. I will probably send her some socks. Maybe some under shirts and maybe a few dollars.

She might like a new hat, since she always wears that black one. I may get her some boots for her birthday or Christmas. That would be nice. I think she would like them. They would be comfortable and I think she would enjoy them for the winter.

Well, that is all. I just wanted to talk about my mother for a few minutes, because I just called her and finally, she said she does not feel like talking to anybody. I have always expected that, but when it finally happened, it made me feel sad. I just needed to vent about it.

August 11, 2018 – *Addendum added on May 16, 2019*

I *did* feel hurt when she did not come to the phone. It was like she did not want us then and she does not want us now. I even processed how I was feeling at that time with my brother, Jerome. He encouraged me to just take her word and believe that she just was not feeling up to coming to the phone.

After all, the worker there told me she was okay, but her hip was hurting. Although that made good sense, all the rejection that I felt over the years came rushing back and overruled the part that made sense.

That was one of the days when I was convinced, telling myself that, "I guess she *really* did not want us."

August 12, 2018

Just thinking about my mother and a part of me says that is cool if she does not to be with us, I haven't been with her all my life anyway. I know she has a mental illness, and that she is happy where she is. I feel like the biggest part of me does not really care. Then, there is that part of me that does care and that is the part of me that is talking right now.

She is in another state and I would love to be able to take care of her by making sure she gets treatment for her hip because she is always in pain. She said she had an x-ray, but never got the results and I believe she cares about herself. She has mentioned wanting to get the care she needs for her hip. It is just that there is nobody taking care of her so she is just walking around with the pain, not really knowing or understanding what is really going on inside of her body.

I wish I could do something about it. For example, I was looking online and saw a hip brace that she can wear around her hip and her leg for support. Then again, what good will a brace do if we are not aware of what is really going on, we do not have a diagnosis.

I am sure it would give her some support and help her to feel better when she walks. I could send her one of those and let her get used to wearing it for a while. Then maybe send another one later when that one wears out. However, it would be nice if I could actually facilitate getting her the medical care she needs.

I do not know if the boarding home takes care of the residents in that way there. I guess I could call and ask, but I do not think that would be a good idea. My mother knows how to express her own wants and needs. If she wants medical care, I am sure she will ask for it.

One might think it would be easy for me to simply say, "I don't care," since she has been gone for so many years. However, that is not the case. I understand that her mental illness caused her to be away, and that it prevents her from fully showing that she cares.

Finding Mother: A Journey of Loss and Love

I believe she cares about family, but not enough to want to live close to us. She loved it when we went to visit her, she could not wait until we got there and she was happy the entire time that we were there. She spent a lot of time with us and was very elated to have us there.

It is just hard to really look after her when she is living there. She is so used to taking care of herself, that I have wondered if she could be afraid to be with us. Because when I mentioned that the place I had in mind for her here would make sure she takes her medication, I noticed she seemed a bit fearful, as if she does not want anyone making sure she takes it.

If I was retired and home all day, I probably would want to take care of her. I could spend time with her. I could take her to the park. I could take her out walking. I could oversee her healthcare. I could just take care of her.

I do not know if they have any mental health treatment centers here like the one she attends.

If she lived with me, I would make sure she has healthy meals, but then she would need to go to some type mental health treatment center all day long when I go to work. Even when I do not go to work, she could go there and get her mental health needs taken care of.

That looks like a good place where she is currently at, offering her the behavioral health care that she needs every single day like that. I do not know of any places like that here where she could actually have that. The boarding home where she is living is not so cool. However, she goes to the center, which seems like a nice place for her to go.

Nevertheless, there is still that feeling of sadness that comes with having met her and she does not want to be with us. She did not even come to the phone yesterday.

I feel like I am not supposed to care.

I feel like I should not care.

A part of me does not.

Finding Mother: A Journey of Loss and Love

Then again, I do.

It is like, I cannot even really have a mother to talk to on the phone. I know she has a mental illness. However, that does not change the disappointment that comes from not being able to have the type of relationship that I would expect I should have with someone who is my mother.

She is so little and such a nice person. I feel badly because she has had to deal with a mental illness for most of her life. I feel badly that she did not have her children in her life.

She did not have her husband, my father, whom she seemed to really look up to and admire.

She said, "He never came" to visit her in the mental hospital, where she stayed for two years. The thought of him never coming makes me feel sad. Her mental illness caused her not to have her family.

It is kind of like she probably would have wanted a family if somebody was taking care of her. My father was not really equipped to take care of mental issues. He needed her to take care of him, the house, and the children. They needed each other, but neither was able to fulfill the needs of the other.

In a way, she may not have allowed him to be able to care for her because she might have been in denial about taking her medication. If he could not get her to take it, then how could he help her to manage her mental illness? I have seen how my sister is, and sometimes you cannot really control a person who has a mental illness.

While a part of me feels like my father should have taken care of her and given her the medication. Another part of me knows my father may not have had that kind of control over my mother.

After she went off to the mental hospital, my father was trying to work and take care of us and I guess he couldn't have the time off to go and visit my mother, especially if he was feeling unwanted. He may have thought, "Why should I push myself upon her?"

Finding Mother: A Journey of Loss and Love

Even now, she is in a good place, but I feel like I have to "pursue" her just to be able to talk to her and do things for her. My father would probably have had to push himself upon her even more so back then. According to my brother, she was in a much worse place back then. I would imagine if she is reluctant to take medication now, she was probably even more reluctant back then.

My father had to call the police to have her committed to a mental hospital. So, I guess that would indicate that she may not have been taking her medication like she should and he could not get her to cooperate so that she could be okay. So, once he got her placed in the mental hospital, he may have just proceeded with his life of raising six children. Keeping track of her progress may have been too much for him.

My father said she could be the sweetest person, but then she could be the total opposite. When this happened, there was really no getting through to her. I guess I can imagine why my father "never came." It is sad and it seems like, "Oh that is too bad. Nobody ever came," you know?

If she were in a mental hospital here, I think I would go visit her because they would be keeping her on her medication. My father was probably not up to taking care of her when he needed so much help himself, that is just my guess.

Anyway, I thank God for my Grandmother. She was there for us, and during my time with her, I saw what it looked like to have a good, decent, normal life. The places where I lived with my father were not so nice. Many times, we did not have food and almost never had a phone. We would have a phone for a short period, then it would get disconnected since no one paid the bill.

I do not remember our utilities being turned off while my father was around. But, after he left us in the house alone, the utilities were disconnected due to nonpayment. I remember not having a phone even with my father around. I remember thinking, "When I grow up and get my own place, I am going to *always* have a phone, and my bills will *always* be paid."

Finding Mother: A Journey of Loss and Love

After my mother left, my grandmother came to see about us a lot. Whenever I was over at my grandmother's house, I had a decent life. I appreciate my grandmother. I have always had nothing but love for her.

Whenever I went to my grandmother's house, there was always food. She brought homemade milkshakes, which she made in the blender, to my bedside before I would go to sleep at night. I guess milk does help people to fall asleep. Sometimes the milkshake would be strawberry, sometimes it would be chocolate, and sometimes it would be vanilla. Strawberry was my favorite!

She showed me what it was like to have all the necessities and a fulfilled life; and what it was like to have someone to really, really look out for me. She completely looked out for me, she took care of me, and all of my needs: physical and social.

She took me places, like out of town with her. She enrolled me in school and drove me to kindergarten when I was only four years old. My grandmother had taught me my ABCs, numbers, and shapes. Therefore, the school let me enroll early because I had taken the early entrance test.

Grandmother would never allow me to eat at fast food restaurants. It was she who showed me what it was really like for someone to be nice to you, to have everything you want and need, to have somebody teach you the things that you need, to buy you toys that are fun and educational. She was the only one who taught me what it felt like to be a well-rounded person. I credit her for that. I would not have even known what all of that looked like had it not been for her.

I want to say, I was not with her long enough to reap the full benefits; but then again, my mother was with her all of her life, and my mother still ended up dealing with mental illness, and becoming opposite of what my grandmother taught her. Therefore, I am not sure if the amount of time I was with her is relevant.

Yeah, it would be nice to have my mother here, so that I could serve her some heathy meals and oversee her medication. I could get her the care she needs for her hip. I could take her to her medical appointments. Maybe in addition to taking her out for walks, I could take her to the park. I could take her to get her hair done, to get manicures and pedicures, take her to church. It is nice to think about all the ways I could take care of her, but it seems she is doing fine right where she is.

It sounds like she could possibly have her own room at the place where she is right now if she could live on the second floor. But, she needs to be on the first-floor due to her hip pain.

I guess she does not necessarily have to be here in Kansas City with us. If she just had her own room then maybe she would not have to carry her stuff around. What are the chances of her getting her own room though? I wish there was a way that I could make things better for her while she is there, but that would just be a lot for me to take on.

Maybe I will just go ahead and send her the hip brace. I do not know if that will work for her or not. I wish she knew what was going on in her hip area. It could be arthritis and she could possibly need surgery. It could be just a matter of physical therapy and she could be all better. I guess she needs to find out the results of the x-ray that she had. If she only needs physical therapy then the brace may actually be helpful.

Anyway, enough of that. I do not know if I want to initiate taking on responsibility for her. Especially since she has not requested it…also, since she does not want to be with us, *and* since she does not really care to come to the phone when I call. Anyway, that is all I need to say for now.

August 22, 2018

    I would really be happy to learn more about my mother's life story. I was reading my foster care story, *A Gifted Child in Foster Care*, for the first time since finding my mother. As I read the book, I was just kind of reminiscing on how I felt as I wrote that story, compared to how I feel now after meeting my mother. I was reading some of the things I wrote about her, the things I remember when I was only two, and then thinking about her now and trying to imagine her actually doing those things that I remember.

    I even wrote a part in the book about never being able to find her and finally giving up, because I really had given up. I truly did not think I would be able to find her at the time that I wrote my foster care story.

    Finding her has just put a completely different view on the situation. I have peace, contentment, and comfort; and I feel empowered. All of those things just for finding her and seeing who she really is, and getting a good look for myself at her mental illness that she had before she left, that I did not even recognize back then.

    For example, in my foster care story, I did not know why she seemed so "slow" and told me that I had to take a bath before I could have those cookies that she made, but then it seemed like she did not even care, or have any motivation, to make sure I got any of the cookies. I mean, she did not put any aside for me, and she gave me my bath so slow and she left all the cookies with all of the other children. She did not seem to have any understanding that I probably was not going to get any of those cookies even though she told me I could have some after I took my bath.

    Seeing her now helps me to understand that. It is like "Okay, now I see," but at the time it just did not make sense to me why I missed out on those cookies.

    I still cannot believe that woman is my mother. However, like I said, I want to learn more about her life story. I would like to put the pieces together and learn about her life as a little girl. Like,

Finding Mother: A Journey of Loss and Love

when did she realize she had mental illness? I would really like to know her story.

The question is, will I be able to get the pieces that I need in order to know her story?

Will she talk to me?

Is she able open up to me?

Because when it comes to things that are stressful, and things about her life, she closes up and she does not like to talk about it. Then again, maybe her life has not been as stressful as I may think.

She said she was married for two years after she left us and I am wondering what happened after that. She still has that man's last name.

Did they just leave each other but stayed married?

Did she get a divorce and keep his name?

Did he remarry?

Did he have more kids?

I would really like to know more.

I mean she just might open up. It may be therapeutic for her to talk more about her life. She may get a sense of peace from talking about it.

I would like to learn more about her story from a little girl until adulthood, including from the time she left us until where she is today.

I know some things, but there is so much that is still missing.

August 22, 2018

What do I actually know about my mother's story? From what I gather, my mother was adopted when she was two years old. Her birth mother had about seven children and she was not taking care of any of them because she had a mental illness. The state had taken them all way. My mother was the only one still living with her.

My grandmother told me that my mother's mother did not want her, and she told my grandmother to "take her." So, my grandmother took her. Knowing her mother had the same illness as her, I understand why Grandmother would just take her like that. My mother probably would have ended up in foster care or adopted by somebody anyway.

Now it all makes sense. I believe my grandmother did what she had to do in the situation. She could not have children of her own. She saw this cute little neglected girl, and took the steps necessary to have this little girl so she could take care of her.

My grandmother took care of my mother and it sounds like she treated my mother similar to how she treated me. She taught her things, like how to play the piano. Grandmother always bragged that my mother was a great piano player and that she was smart. Grandmother dressed her up and took all kind of pictures of her.

I know the city and state where my mother was born and where she grew up. She even remembers the address of where they lived. She grew up with her blood uncle and his wife, which is the woman whom I called Grandmother. She called her uncle Father and she called my grandmother Mother.

My grandmother raised my mother properly. She taught her proper etiquette for all occasions. My grandmother wanted her to be "just as good as anyone else." She had to dress nice, look nice, and talk using correct grammar. That is how my grandmother taught me, too. My Grandmother raised my mother similar to how she raised me during the times I spent with her.

Finding Mother: A Journey of Loss and Love

My mother grew up with my grandmother. I did not know any other details about how she grew up except she was wonderful at playing the piano, and my grandmother raised her to be very prim and proper.

After I found my mother, she told me some additional stories about her life. She told me the story of how she met my father, among other stories (which I have shared in the *Finding Mother Series* of books).

I do not know at what point she began to display her mental illness, or when my father learned about it. Did he notice it? Had it begun to show itself around the time they first met? I know she was a pretty woman though, so maybe he could not tell. Maybe it had not manifested during that time. She may have looked so "normal" back then that he just could not imagine she would have a mental illness and that it could be so serious. That could be the case.

I would like to know about her life from the time she lived with my grandmother until the time she married my father. When did it become obvious that she had a mental illness to the point that it was affecting her life in such a major way? I would really like to know that.

So anyway, she met my dad and, at some point, they got married. I do not know the details of their dating process, from after their meeting up until their marriage. The next thing I know about my mother is that she married my father and they moved around a lot. As they moved from place to place, they had Jerome, then Grayson, Carla, Terrance, and Danisha. Then I was born.

They ended up in Kansas City, to be close to my grandmother. They needed her help because, by that time, my mother's mental illness was adversely affecting the family. Kansas City is where my mother ultimately ran away from, leaving my father to raise six children alone.

According to my father, she never took her birth control pills the way she should have. He was upset about that. He often complained after she left that she did not believe in birth control and she did not believe in abortion, yet she never wanted that many children.

During my second visit with my mother, she told me she was on birth control pills but she still ended up pregnant time after time. She ultimately gave birth to ten children. Six with my father and four with Calvin, the man she ran away with.

On another note, she told me a story of something that had happened before she left us. One day when she came home on a furlough from the mental hospital, her children were all telling her that my father had brought a girlfriend over. She said she never said anything to him about it. Her story made me feel like she suspected my father of cheating but she never asked him about it.

She said she never questioned him about what he did when he was away from home either. She said she just loved him and that she taught her children to love him too, no matter what. She told me she learned a long time ago that if you looked for trouble you would find it. Therefore, she never looked for anything bad because he was good to her so she just appreciated that. I was surprised to hear her say that. I felt like that was her way of using wisdom.

My mom seems like she was nonchalant and did not worry about her relationship with my father. It seems she just enjoyed her marriage. It seems she relished the good part and ignored the bad part. I do not know if that is good or bad but that is how she dealt with it. Sadly, she ended up losing my father anyway because he put her in a mental hospital and never came back to visit her. I feel disappointed in my father for doing that.

On a side note, during my second visit with my mother, she mentioned she had some good children; she mentioned how Carla was "as cute as a button" when she was born; she mentioned how I was a "real fat baby" and how I was "the cutest thing you ever want to see" when I was born. However, she did not mention any specific details about the births of the rest of my siblings.

I am curious about the details, including her thoughts and feelings, surrounding their births. It is my understanding that

Danisha and I would have ended up in foster care or adopted if my father had not been there to take us home from the hospital.

Perhaps I could learn more about my sibling's births, as well of other aspects of my mother's life, if she and I could have more conversations.

September 9, 2018

So, I am in my feelings about the last time I called my mother and she said she did not feel like talking to anybody. This brings back memories of how my father would tell us that my mother probably would not receive us if we ever found her.

It pains me to admit that he was right. She did not receive us when we first got there. She receives us now, but it is weird because she still seems satisfied without us. She has done a pretty good job trying to make me feel comfortable and trying to make me feel like she actually wants me.

I think she is okay either way. What I mean is, if I want to be in her life, she is okay with it. If I do not, she would be okay with that, too, because she is content the way she is. She left for a reason. She never wanted all of those children. Therefore, she is cool without us at this stage of her life.

In all actuality, I pretty much feel the same way. Even though I am feeling emotional about this, there is still that part of me that feels like she has not been in my life for all of these years, so I am perfectly okay with her not being in my life now.

Finding Mother: A Journey of Loss and Love

September 12, 2018

I am remembering how my mother told me that she volunteered in the children's nursery at the church we used to go to before she abandoned us. For years, I had been sharing a story of how she would come to pick me up from the nursery, and brag to the people there about how smart I was. After I reunited with her, I told her I remembered that story and she confirmed that she actually *volunteered* in the children' nursery. So, she was not merely picking me up.

All of those years when I thought she was picking me up from the nursery, she was actually in there with me because she was volunteering. Even though I vividly remember things about my mother when I was only two years old, there are still parts I do not know. I never would have imagined that she actually volunteered in the nursery.

She does not remember some of the stories that I shared with her. She actually did not even remember the story of bragging about me to the nursery workers. She just remembered that she volunteered in the nursery.

When I asked her if she remembered walking me around to the convenience store and buying me malt balls candy, she did not remember that. She did not remember walking me to the store at all.

I told her I remembered her laying in the grass in the backyard crying, afraid of being taken away. She did not really respond to that. Probably because it was a hurtful moment, and she preferred to talk about things that felt good to her. She has a way of blocking out negative things and only thinking about good and positive things. That seems to be her way of coping with potentially hurtful things in her life.

It is interesting for me to learn her side of some of the memories I have carried around with me for so many years.

I am also thinking about how my mother mentioned wanting to have a coat with pockets on the inside so that she can hide her stuff. That makes sense since she has been robbed. She also mentioned wanting a cell phone and being able to hide it inside of the coat pockets. She probably would hide it and take good care of it.

However, I am still afraid she might lose it or somebody in the boarding home may steal it while she is asleep, or something, because they would know she has it. I am also concerned about her learning how to use it, because it is not the same as using a regular phone. I do not know if she has ever had one before or if she knows anything about how one works. I know that she would really like to have one. However, I do not know if it is a good idea for me to buy her one.

She may be better off obtaining a cell phone from one of those places that provide free cell phones for people who are on a fixed income. Sometimes, those places will provide a phone with a certain number of free minutes per month. That could be an option for her to get started with having a phone, since it is free and we could see how she does with it. I am sure she does not need too many minutes per month anyway.

Now I know for sure that the boarding home will let her call her family long distance from there if she wants to. She just chooses not to. I do not know if they would make a big deal out of it if she did it too much. They probably would.

How do you tell a mentally ill resident they cannot call their family? How do you tell an elderly woman who has lived there for over fifteen years she cannot call her family, especially when all of her income goes to that place?

Well anyway, it would be nice if she had her own room in that place. Then I would probably send her a nice mattress. Maybe even a nice comfortable chair. Those are the things I would want to do for her if she were here, but, not really while she is there.

I guess if she did not have to share a room there, it would not hurt. Since she wants to be there, maybe she could have her own space where residents would not be able to steal from her. Then she can have more without having the worry of her things being stolen. Maybe she could even have a television or a refrigerator in her room.

It would be nice if she could have a better room in the place where she actually wants to be. However, then she would no longer fit in with the other residents at the boarding home. She would no longer have the appearance of someone who is homeless. To me, it just does not seem feasible to provide that type of life for her in the place where she is. That is just not the place to have many things. It's really not.

I wonder if there are any nicer assisted-living homes in her city, where she could live. The only thing about that is that she likes the boarding home and she is used to being there. She probably would not want to live in another place. Considering how she has been conditioned, she could potentially carry all of her belongings around in a backpack even if she moves to an environment where no one steals.

This diary entry started with me talking about her working in the church nursery and how she does not remember the stories that I remember. When I told her about when I used to go into her closet and put on her clothes and shoes, I imagined she may have chastised me for it, because she used to take me out of her closet. Then, as soon as she was not looking, I would go right back in there.

When I mentioned that memory to her during my visit, she had a look on her face that told me that was not a cute memory for her. It was as if she was thinking, "Oh, you remember that?" Her reaction made me wonder if maybe she disciplined me for it and I just do not remember that part.

I am in awe about how I witnessed my mother being beaten by my father, then listened to her as she denied it forty-nine years later. She made excuses for my father, saying he treated her good. She said he never did anything for her to be angry with him about. When in reality he admitted to beating her and it was not right. It was not fair to her.

Finding Mother: A Journey of Loss and Love

Then again, if he hit her for harming us, the way Jerome said, then maybe she understands why he did it and therefore, maybe she honestly is not angry with him. I remember my oldest sister, Carla beating up on our sister, Danisha, who has the same mental illness as my mother, for trying to beat up on me.

So maybe that is just what my family did, protected each other. My father protected us from my mother. He did all he could to protect us, and to try to keep us together. For example, bringing me home from the hospital at birth, when my mother was in the mental hospital. That really was honorable of him.

My foster care caseworker used to tell me that my father really cared about us; and that he was doing all he could to keep us together. I did not understand what she meant back then. Now I do. He must have told them the story, like the whole story, including how my mother left me in the hospital.

My father never told me that my mother left me in the hospital and that he brought me home. I had never heard that story. I figured it out when I got my birth records. When I looked at my records, I thought, "Wow, it looks like my father took me home from the hospital!" Then my mother confirmed it when I met her. I had heard he brought Danisha home from the hospital, too.

So now, I can see how he tried to keep us together. I used to wonder how he could have possibly been trying to keep us together if he left us in that house alone, and we ended up in foster care. But, now, I am able to look beyond the fact that he put his big old hands on my little bitty mother, and recognize his sincere efforts to do what he thought was best for his children.

September 15, 2018

I am feeling kind of upset. I feel like I called my mother too soon from the last time. The last time I called was to let her know I had sent her a package and to tell her to expect it last Thursday. She said she was going to call me Thursday to let me know she received it. She did not call me.

I ended up calling her again today just to confirm the package had arrived. I really did not want to speak to her, but the boarding home worker called her to the phone. I did not want to overwhelm her by the frequency of my calls. She did not call me Thursday but I called her today because I really wanted to know if the package got there okay.

To my dismay, the worker went to get her, then came back to the phone and told me she was not coming to the phone. I said okay and we hung up. A couple of minutes later, I decided to call back to find out why she was not coming to the phone, and another worker answered.

It was April, and she exclaimed, "She needs to come to the phone!" After she had confirmed that I was the daughter who was sending her the package, she sounded infuriated. "Most families of the people here don't care anything about them! I am going to go get her because she needs to come to the phone!"

After a few moments of silence where April went to get Mother, she came back and explained that my mother could not come because her hip was hurting. But, otherwise she was okay.

A part of me wondered if my mother might be using that as an excuse. However, I know that her hip is always hurting. It could be hurting more now than normal. She could not feel like getting up because of it. That could very well be the case, I guess. I remember when we wanted to take her out for dinner and she was concerned about "hopping" into the restaurant. I took that to mean she was concerned because her hip hurts a lot. I guess she does not have to come to the phone if she is in pain. I should not expect it.

Still, I asked myself, "Is her hip really hurting that badly, or is this a sign that she still does not want me after all of these years?"

What if the true reason that she did not come to the phone was because of her hip pain just like she said? What if she truly just did not feel like getting up walking with so much pain? If that is absolutely the reason then I would have to accept that as her reason.

She said she would call me tomorrow. I do not know if I believe that but I just have to take her word. If she does not call me tomorrow then I will know, "Okay, she did not call me."

April said she would be sure to have her to call me tomorrow. We will see. Otherwise, I am almost tempted to give up trying to have an ongoing relationship with her. I understand that she has a serious mental illness, but understanding that heartbreaking fact does not stop the pain associated with it.

I remember how father and grandmother told me my mother did not want me. Now, I actually see it for myself. They told me the truth but I did not realize it. I felt disappointed with them for telling me that my mother did not want me. I thought, "How can you just tell a child her mother did not want her?" I thought, there's no way my mother did not want me. I thought they were just telling me that.

No, they were serious. They were telling me the truth. My mother did not want me. I can see that now. I mean, I know she enjoys knowing me. She even made a joke about me when we were looking at pictures during my second visit. We were looking at a picture of Arica and I. She said Arica was very pretty in the picture, then she looked at me in the picture and said, "You are *alright*." Then she laughed and we all laughed. I thought it was cute that she knew how to make that kind of joke and that she was comfortable joking with me in that manner.

I know she doesn't dislike me. She just never wanted so many children, and since she has been on her own for so long, she is happier that way.

Finding Mother: A Journey of Loss and Love

September 16, 2018

I am just lying here on my bed before I fall asleep, contemplating how my mother did not come to the phone when I called yesterday. I had talked to her and told her I sent her a package. She told me she was going to call me when it arrived on Thursday and let me know that she got it. She did not do that.

Then I called her to confirm whether or not it was delivered and she did not come to the phone. I do not know if she got the package. I looked up the tracking number and it looked like the center director, Donna, received the delivery.

So, it looked like it was received. I guess I just wanted to know for sure for if the package actually reached my mother's hands. April had said she would make sure Mother called me today, but I did not receive that call. This makes me wonder if it would be easier if I did not know where she was, than to know where she is and feel unwanted by her.

Once, when I sent her something, she told me it was sweet of me to think of her like that. That made me feel like she did not really see me as her daughter who feels obligated to look after her, but like she saw me as a friend who does not owe her anything. I saw her as my mother, someone who I should be taking care of. She just did not seem to feel the same way.

However, one time we were talking on the phone and I told her I was not feeling well. She immediately started giving me pointers about how to take care of myself, you know, like a mother would do. I just said, "Yeah," as if to tell her, "I already know how to take care of myself." I felt surprised that her motherly instinct actually stepped up in that moment.

My first instinct was to feel like I did not need a mother. In a way, I felt honored that she showed that she cared. In another way, it felt unusual for her to act "motherly" towards me after being away for my entire life.

So, I am thinking about how she did not come to the phone and did not call me back as she promised. I am seriously considering not ever calling her again because she does not seem interested. Then again, that may be what happened with her and my father. She said he never came.

I am wondering if he could have possibly felt the same way I am feeling right now, and if that could have possibly been the reason why he gave up on her. I would hate for her to experience the same rejection from me that she experienced from my father. However, I am afraid I may approach another point in my life where I will have to say, "Well, if she don't want me, I don't want her *needer*."

That could also be why neither he, nor my grandmother, took us to visit her in the mental hospital leading up to her disappearance. My father seemed to have known she would not receive us, so taking us to see her might have been more harmful for us than helpful. She may not have really cared to have us visit since, according to her, she was in the hospital because she needed a break from all of her children.

Therefore, taking us to visit her may have been counter-productive for her. Besides, I believe that if she really wanted to see us, she would have come for us after she left the hospital, before running off with Calvin. She also knew the city and state where she left us, so she could have always come back to find us if she wanted.

I believe she actually remembers a whole lot more surrounding the time she ran away from Kansas City. I think she may feel ashamed of not wanting us. She admitted wanting a "break" from us, however. So, I can appreciate her being honest with me about that. Back then, we were little children who may have been a burden to her. It may have been hard for her to imagine, at that time, that we would one day be grown-ups who would no longer need her.

Well anyway, I have a decision to make. I have to decide if I am going to continue to try to reach out to her when it seems as if she does not really care about that. I feel torn between continuing to call her and stopping calling her. I guess I could talk to April about it first. April would probably say, "Just keep calling her," because she needs family even if she does not act as if she does.

It would be nice for me to be able to call her every once in a while, just to talk to her. It would be nice if I could continue to send her things, just because she is my mother, just because she gave birth to me. However, it would also be nice to be able to confirm she received what I sent, and to know whether she liked it.

For example, I wonder if she likes the yarn and knitting needles I sent. I wonder if she is actually knitting. Maybe when I ask April about whether or not I should continue to call my mother, I can also ask her if the knitting supplies were helpful for her. That is, if she even received the package. I was hoping the knitting supplies could be a source of therapy since her counselor told me she shared her desire to knit in a group therapy session. It would mean a lot to me if she were actually knitting.

However, for the most part, my mission is accomplished. I found her, I know where she is and I know what she is like. She does not seem interested in being a mother or a grandmother. I mean, she told my daughter, Arica, to call her Geneva.

I do not know what it would have been like to grow up with her. I have always wondered, "What would be worse? Her staying in Kansas City, but being in a mental hospital? Her being in the home with us, but doing things to harm us? Never finding her and not knowing anything about her condition? Or finding her after all these years, the way we did, but not really being able to have a relationship with her due to her mental illness?'

I guess my choice would be to know her, but I realize I am not going to have a mother in the way that I would like to.

The least I wanted was some occasional conversation. I originally wanted to talk to her a lot and listen to her talk. I wanted to learn a lot about her life; what she likes and what her life has been like for all the years she has been gone. I learned her story of why she left, but I still do not know where she has been all of these years.

Finding Mother: A Journey of Loss and Love

After going back to visit her for a second time and seeing how hard it was for her talk about why she left, I resolved to accept the fact that I may never know what she did with her life from the time she left until the time we found her. I mean, I know she married Calvin. I know she had four more children, all of whom she left in a hospital. I know she mentioned living with a family for eight years.

I wanted to ask her for more details about living with that family, but she did not seem like she wanted to expound on it, so I did not ask. I know that she has been living at the boarding home for over fifteen years now. However, I am oblivious to any other details concerning where she has been since she abandoned us forty-nine years ago. I am guessing she spent many of those years committed to a mental hospital, but I do not really know.

Our situation is somewhat unfortunate, but at least I was fortunate enough to have found her. For years, I prayed to find her. I always felt in my heart that I would find her one day. I had even had a dream once about my siblings and I going to another state together to reunite with her, and that actually ended up happening!

Therefore, I got my wish, which was to find her before she passed away. I feel like I should just simply be happy with that, especially if she is satisfied where she is and she is okay. She complains about the boarding home residents stealing from her. She is content to be there though and she does not want to leave.

I mean, I have a choice. I can leave her alone and say, "Okay, she is happy," or I can continue to acknowledge her for holidays. I sent the last package "just because." There was no holiday or special occasion. Regardless of what I decide to do, it would still be nice to know how she felt about that last package I sent or if she even received it.

Maybe I will call Donna and ask her, since she would have been the one who gave it to her. I mean, my mother knows how to call me and tell me, but it does not seem like she is going to do that.

Finding Mother: A Journey of Loss and Love

As Terrance once said, "It would be nice if *she* would give *us* a call." It would let us know that she wants to talk to us.

I feel like giving up.

Besides, why should I keep sending her things when people who live with her are just going to steal it from her? If she has many things in a place where other residents have nothing, it would make her a very large target. Therefore, it may actually be best for her, too, if I stop sending stuff.

So anyway, I guess I have said enough for now. Basically, I wanted to talk out my feelings about her not coming to the phone yesterday, her not calling me back like she promised, and about not really knowing the status of the package that I sent.

September 17, 2018

I am having thoughts about my father and the way he acted after my mother left the family. My father was very protective over my siblings and me. Now, I understand why. I now understand his struggle.

Over the years, my oldest brother often shared his own anger about how people treated us and how my father stood up for us. The full details of what my brother shared with me are his own story to tell. However, my point is this: I never fully understood his anger and I never fully understood my father's commitment to us until I met and talked to my mother.

As I was growing up, whenever I would speak of my disappointment about my father beating my mother, my brother would say, "Grace, our mother really did have a mental illness and our father didn't cause it." Even though my brother explained that to me on numerous occasions over the years, I continued to believe that my father was the reason my mother left, and that he somehow caused her mental illness to manifest itself more largely that it would have if it were not for the way he treated her.

I do think she may have lived a better life if she had only had the two children that she wanted, and if my father had not expected more from her as a wife than she was capable of giving. Did he have a right to expect those things? I guess so. I believe we all have our expectations of what we want from a mate and so did my father. Unfortunately, my mother was unable to deliver.

I believe that the pressure from my father for her to deliver caused more stress on her mental condition. It seemed my father did not really understand her mental illness and the full effects of it on a large family. It seems I misunderstood my father's challenge of not having my mother as the helpmate that he so desperately longed for and desired.

When I reviewed my birth records a second time, after finding my mother, I realized the hardship my father must have experienced having to take me home and care for me without the help of my mother.

Mother confirmed she was in a mental hospital when I was born, which is why my father took me home from the hospital. This part really makes me realize the investment my father had in me, how much he cared, how much he loved me, the hardships he experienced just to keep us together, and the pain of not having help from our mother to raise us.

He was already struggling to raise five children with a mentally ill wife, when I was born. Yet he was still committed to bringing me home from the hospital to keep his family together.

Meeting my mother and talking to her has helped me to better understand my father's struggles, his justifications, his hurt, his anger, and why he was so very protective of my siblings and I. He even protected us against our mentally ill mother. I realized my father had a lot vested in me and my siblings, and I now believe that is why my father was so protective of me as I was growing up.

He *always* took my side even when I was wrong. If an outsider came knocking on our door to tell him of something I did wrong, he would tell them they needed to be focusing on their own children instead of telling him about his. I would never get in trouble when outsiders would snitch on me.

However, in my heart, I would feel lucky that my father became angry with them instead of punishing me for what they said I had done and I would be sure, within myself, to do better next time.

I am considering what my father must have went through with my mother, while trying to raise six children. Before meeting her and talking with her, I had always blamed him for her leaving. I understand now. I realize what he went through with our mother.

I thought he was just making excuses when he was talking badly about her, saying how she had mental illness, that she never did anything for us, saying she did not want us, and mocking her for saying, "One day, I am going to go far, far away." Furthermore, how he was afraid that she would not receive us if we ever found her. I had always thought he was just angry. Even though he may have actually been angry in part, I now understand his plight.

When he would say he had to knock some sense into her, I did not understand that. Now I do. I am not saying I agree with him hitting her, but I understand his thought process now.

It is weird because he never physically abused my siblings or me. But, somehow, he thought his beatings would cause her to act the way he wanted her to. He thought that she just needed a good whooping. I guess he thought she was kind of like a child, and that if he just gave her a good whooping that she would do better.

Obviously, that did not work. After meeting and talking with her, it appears she may have understood his actions, because she said he treated her nice.

So maybe he talked with her about it before and after. Maybe she understood that he was hitting her because she had harmed one of us. I have reason to believe he may have also beat her when she did not have dinner ready and the house was dirty when he came home from work.

That is just something I was told. I do not specifically remember that, so it is only hearsay. However, I do remember him complaining about her being home all day and not cooking, cleaning or even getting dressed. I just do not remember if he actually beat her for it.

Nevertheless, I now understand how my father must have felt to have a wife who had a mental illness, who was not able to be a mother, who was unable do anything for the children, and who did not even want that many children. I wonder if my mother ever imagined that the day would arrive that we would come to reunite with her.

Well, that day came and I am thankful because she finally received us after our very long trip. We had sacrificed way too much to go there to reunite with her, for her to proclaim she did not know who we were.

Finding Mother: A Journey of Loss and Love

After she finally accepted us, she said she loves family. I guess a part of her wants family, but a part of her has become satisfied with not having us. The fact that she does not want to come live closer, and the fact that she never initiates phone calls to us, reminds me of how she did not want us back then.

It makes me feel like she still does not want us now.

She may or may not feel that way, but that is how I feel.

However, I am still not sure if the words, "your mother does not want you," were the best thing for my father and grandmother to say to me as a two-year-old child, even if it may have been the truth.

Perhaps something like, "your mother has a mental illness, she does not know how to love you, and she is not able to take care of you," would have been a better way to tell me. Either way I would have felt hurt, so I am not sure if a different wording would have decreased the rejection I felt for most of my life.

Now that I truly understand my father did not in any way cause my mother's mental illness, I am guessing it is simply hereditary because her birth mother had a mental illness. One of my sisters has the exact same mental illness, too.

My father never told my sister she had an illness, and he never sought treatment for her. He just always treated her as if she was very special. I believe he thought he could just be nice to her and she would be okay. His plan did not work. The last time I saw my sister, she was in denial about having a diagnosed mental illness. Therefore, she was not taking any medication to relieve her very serious symptoms.

My feelings still remain mixed.

Should I call my mother again?

Should I just leave her be?

Is she pushing me away because she really wants me to go away?

Would she push me away, then be sad that I am gone?

If I go away, would she feel hurt like nobody cares?

Finding Mother: A Journey of Loss and Love

Would it be better for her if I were not pursuing a relationship with her?

I feel she has been very gracious to us. After all, the only things we ever wanted was to be nice to her, to love her, and take care of her if she would allow it.

On another note, I still want to know what her life was like before she ended up living there.

Did she meet other men after her two-year marriage ended with Calvin?

Had she been homeless on the streets?

Had she been locked away in a mental hospital?

What happened after those two years?

I wish I could ask her.

However, things that happened after she left seemed to be the things that she is most uncomfortable talking about. The good thing about her is that she tries to hold on to all the good memories.

Like the way she stared at the picture of herself standing outside of her childhood home. I am guessing that picture reminded her of the good old days when her life was pleasant. She shies away from talking about hurtful memories.

While finding her has helped me to know more about her than I did before, I still wish I could know more. She seemed to avoid talking too much about Calvin, the man who she ran away with. She said he had family out of town. He, too, had a mental illness but it seems she trusted him to provide for her.

I guess if she had stayed with us, she would have been expected to be a wife and mother and she did not know how. She would have had to be someone who she was not capable of being.

I believe she saw us, her children, as stressors, burdens. We represented something that caused her grief, something from which she needed to get away.

So, I felt a little bit jealous during my second visit with her. I was sitting in the living room, at the boarding home, talking with my mother. One of the boarding home workers walked into the

Finding Mother: A Journey of Loss and Love

living room with her son. He looked to be around ten or eleven years old. She walked him over to my mother.

She said, "Geneva, do you remember my son, Tommy?"

My mother said, "Oh, wow! Is that Tommy? My how he has grown!"

I was surprised to see this.

The worker was able to share *her* son with *my* mother, who left us as little children. My mother had the capacity to appreciate and enjoy the growth of this little boy.

It really made me feel some kind of a way that this worker knew my mother would be happy to see her son.

It showed me that my mother was a real person, who is able to add joy to the life of someone else, even after running away from her own family.

September 30, 2018

Taking a moment to appreciate some of the things my brother, Jerome, shared with me about our mother. He told me that when we were growing up, she was excellent with sewing, knitting, cooking, and playing the piano. He said whenever she was taking her medication properly, that she was good at all of those things. He believes she is probably still great at those things today. He does not believe she has lost those special talents. I thought that was interesting.

My grandmother had also told me how talented my mother was. She used to tell me about the piano more than anything else. I do not really remember my grandmother telling me about her sewing, knitting, or cooking. Jerome said our mother's cooking was homemade, from scratch, and delicious!

Knowing those things that she is good at makes me want to bring her to Kansas City and get her involved in those things that she loves, maybe buy her a piano and a sewing machine.

October 5, 2018

When someone in your family has a mental illness, it is easy to say, "I am going to look past their behavior because I understand that they have a mental illness."

Nevertheless, that does not take away the pain that comes with not having the type of relationship that you would like to have with them.

Sometimes, I wonder what is harder: living without a mother and not knowing her, or knowing her and having to live with the reality of her mental illness.

October 6, 2018

Before I found my mother, I used to think about how horrible it was for me that my mother left and I never knew where she was, and that I did not have a mother.

I used to wonder, why do I have to go through this heart-wrenching situation?

Why me?

Why did this happen to me of all people?

It just did not seem real that this happened to me.

I felt like my mother was not supposed to leave to me, that these types of things only happen to other people and not me.

Sometimes I wonder how my life would have been had I grown up knowing her. What if she would have remained in the mental hospital in Kansas City and I would have been able to visit her periodically?

I believe it may have still been hard not having her at home. I would have likely felt responsible for her, starting at a very young age. Therefore, I think it is better for me that she was out of my life completely. It gave me a chance to have a more normal childhood.

Even still to this day, I sometimes find myself wondering why *my* mother left *me,* why I had to grow up not having a mother, why I still do not have a mother even though I have found her.

On another note, when she was home, my father could no longer leave us alone with her. She told me how, at one time, he would often go out of town for work, leaving her alone with us. That reminded me of the time when he left my siblings and I in that house alone, so that he could go work in Florida, and we ended up being taken into foster care.

I realize now that was not his first time leaving his family in that manner. In reality, he had stopped traveling for five years (when I was ages two through seven) to stay with us and to try to keep us together. However, that was the first time he left us completely alone, without an adult being in the home with us. So, I am guessing he could not contain his "travel bug" any longer.

Finding Mother: A Journey of Loss and Love

On yet another note, I feel disappointed and heartbroken that even though I found my mother, I still do not really have a mother. I believe my brothers realized that immediately, but it took me some time to understand it. I always imagined that she wanted us back then, and that maybe she tried to take us with her.

I sometimes envisioned my father telling her, "You are not taking my children anywhere!"

Causing her to leave without us.

Then I would wonder, "Well, if she wanted us, then why hasn't she tried to find us?" I even imagined that if we ever found her, she would tell us her story and it would sound something like this:

"Yeah, I did want you all. I tried to take you all with me, but your father would not let me."

Her story was nothing like that.

Her intention was to leave all of us with our father and never have to worry about us again. The good thing, the great thing, the wonderful thing, the blessing is that I was able to find her, to see her, and now my longing has been satisfied.

When I first found her, I was ready to bring her to Kansas City and take care of her without thinking twice about it. Later, when it seemed she was not being clear about whether or not she wanted to come, I began to think about it.

I thought about how, if she were to come, I would be taking care of someone who I do not really know. Someone who did not even want me when I was a little girl. I thought that if she does not want to come, then that would free me from a potentially challenging experience.

Had she agreed to come be with us, I would be taking care of a woman who did not raise me and who was not with me all of my life.

Ironically, however, if she were to call today and say, "I want to come," I would surely begin making arrangements because she is still my mother, so if she actually *wants* to be with us, I would be happy to have her. My brothers and I promised her that if she ever decided to come just let us know and we would make it happen. So, we would keep our promise.

In reality, she does not want to come so I often remind myself that she is in a good place. All of her basic needs are being met. If we had never found her, she would have been okay. I wanted her here with us just in case something serious happened to her then she would be close enough for all of us to be able to help her.

If something serious happens to her while she is there, they may just have to take care of it the way they would if we had not found her. I am grateful to have found her, to have met her, to see what she is like, to have pictures with her, to be able to do some things for her, to have a better understanding of her mental illness and why she left. I am happy to know she is in a stable place where she has been long-term, and she is not living on the streets. I can rest in the fact that this situation is the best it can be.

Now, I am thinking about how my mother did not keep her promise to call me after I sent the package to her.

I know she is very aware of dates, days, and times; and she remembers things very well. Like when Arica and I were scheduled to visit her, she kept asking, "Are you and Arica still coming on June 7th?" Then she would say, "You know Mother's Day is coming up on May 13th?" Then if I called her on a holiday, she would ask, "Are you having a good 4th of July? Did you spend time with your daughter?" Like when Arica and I were there and we came to get her for dinner earlier than she expected, she said, "You all came early." In addition, she gets up in the morning, gets ready for the center, and arrives to the bus on time.

She knows times and days very well.

Therefore, she knows that she said she was going to call me when she got the package and she knows that she did not do it.

After I ended up calling her, she said she would call me back the next day. She did not. When she failed to keep her promises to call me back, I was thinking that maybe her mental illness caused her to forget. In reality, I find it hard to believe that she forgets, which causes me to wonder why she did not call.

That is why I am considering if it would be best for me to simply back away. To think, all my life I had imagined finding my mother and taking care of her.

Finding Mother: A Journey of Loss and Love

October 8, 2018

You know, I could actually cry about my mother, however, I probably will not.

It is difficult finding her, but not really having her. Calling her and her not coming to the phone and not ever calling me.

Over the years, I do not think I have ever cried about not having my mother. I handled my perceived rejection in a different way. My feelings often turned in to heartfelt poems and songs.

I was somewhat silent about it, but I never cried.

Even when they told me she left and did not want me, I did not cry. So why would I start crying about her now? I guess I can think about how unfortunate the situation is. I guess I can allow tears to well up in my eyes. I guess if I ever want to cry, I can just go ahead and do it without holding back.

However, for right now, there is nothing for me to cry about.

I mean, she is okay.

She is a strong woman.

She is probably a lot stronger than I'll ever be in this lifetime. She has been out there. She knows the streets. She was robbed on the streets. Now, she is afraid and I feel sad about that.

That is something I could cry about because I had no idea I would find her living like that. I expected she would be safe and secure in a mental hospital, not able to talk. I never imagined her being out there walking the streets.

She does not really walk the streets anymore.

She is actually living a pretty basic life, going outside on the front step; smoking her cigarettes; eating breakfast, lunch, and dinner; going to bed; getting up; going to the center; talking to people. I mean, she has a real life. She is strong enough to take care of herself.

She looked to my dad to take care of her back then. Then, she looked to Calvin to take care of her when she left. Now, she is taking care of herself.

Therefore, there is no need for me to cry.

October 26, 2018

I have some characteristics that are similar to my mother even though I have not been around her all of my life.

The way she says "Oh, wow!"

I have always said that and so does my daughter. The way we say it is the exact way she says it. As I pondered on how I began to say that in the exact tone as my mother, I wondered how I could have possibly picked that up from her. Then I remembered my sister Carla used to say, "Oh, wow!" all the time.

There is a good possibility that she is the one from whom I copied it. Carla was the oldest girl and she was eight years old when our mother left. I am guessing that she would have been more likely to pick it up from our mother, and I, most likely, picked it up from her.

Our "Oh, wow!" Is probably not hereditary. It is probably environmental. I was able to see a few other characteristics that I have similar to my mother. However, since she was not around as I was growing up I wonder if I inherited from her, or if I picked them up from her before she left, or if my sister picked them up from her and I picked them up from my sister.

November 1, 2018

I kind of want to go see my mother again because I want my son to meet her. I think it is important for him to meet her. At first, I thought we would bring her here and all of her grandchildren would meet her at that time. Now, I do not think she will ever come here.

The thought of moving there has occurred to me. It was only a passing thought, however. I do not actually foresee that ever happening. Besides, I do not think she would welcome that close of a relationship anyway. She has been on her own for a very long time and, actually, so have I. It would probably be uncomfortable for us both.

She has been living her life and she does not really need anyone. Sometimes, I feel like I want to take on a more active role. For example, she would say to me, "I need this." or "I want that." I would provide it, so that she would never feel like she does not have what she needs or wants.

It looks like her basic needs are already being cared for. The boarding home washes her clothes regularly, and they distribute her medication. I would love to do more things for her that she wants. However, having more things would surely cause her to stand out among the other residents at the boarding home. It could make her an even wider target for the residents to continue to steal her stuff.

Sometimes, I think about the fact that there is actually another Geneva living in the same boarding home where my mother, Geneva, lives. The other Geneva actually has my mother's maiden name. So, on the day I found my mother, if I would have asked for her maiden name, the other Geneva may have come to the phone and I may have thought I had found the wrong Geneva and given up looking.

Thankfully, I asked for the correct last name and the right Geneva came to the phone. When she came to the phone, her voice did not sound the way I expected, however, I later realized it did sound a lot like the voice my father would often mock for her. He

Finding Mother: A Journey of Loss and Love

had her voice down pat. I guess she has the same voice now as she had forty-nine years ago. I just did not actually remember her voice.

I have pondered the idea of bringing my mother to live in my home with me. That, too, is nothing more than a passing thought. Since she and I do not really know each other, that would likely not be a good decision.

Sometimes, I think that if I could have a job working at home, then I could take care of her because I would be home all the time. However, she would still require a place to go every day to get the behavioral therapy she needs. Whenever I ponder this idea, I think about a mental health nurse coming into the home to assist with that. Sometimes, I feel like I could handle taking care of her long-term. Other times, I feel like I would be getting in way over my head.

Sometimes, I think about what April and Donna said about as long as she takes her medication, she is okay. Other times, I realize caring for her may be a challenge, for which I am not prepared. Hearing April say, "If she were my mother, I would have her living with me," is what gave me the idea that maybe I could be successful with taking care of her. However, April is a trained professional in the field and I am not.

This part of the diary entry is just a representation of the many times I have thought about having my mother live with me. I do not see that as ever being a real possibility. However, it is interesting for me to think about it from time to time.

November 20, 2018

I am having afterthoughts about our reunion. Grayson, Terrance and myself went back to the boarding home the very next day to have dinner with our mother; and we took chicken. My brother Jerome declined the opportunity to go back. His initial intentions were to go there, see our mother, enjoy her, take a picture or two to share the wonderful memory with his son and maybe our nieces and nephews.

My intentions were different. I wanted to spend every moment that I could with her while we were there, and then try to get her to come back with us so we could take care of her and build a relationship.

I think Jerome just automatically knew what we were up against and I did not. I thought Mother would jump at the opportunity to be with us if only she knew that my father was no longer around. I had always thought she left because of how he treated her. I never would have expected that she left of her own accord and that she wanted to be gone.

Finding Mother: A Journey of Loss and Love

November 22, 2018

I called my mother today. When I told her today was my birthday, she sang the "Happy Birthday" song to me. I thought that was nice of her. She sang… "Happy birthday to you, happy birthday to you, happy birthday dear Grace, happy birthday to you."

I could picture her with a wide smile on her face.

I had never heard my own mother sing "Happy Birthday" to me in my entire life. I had assorted feelings throughout the song.

During this phone call, I finally got a chance to talk to my mother about the package I sent. She confirmed she had received it. She said she likes the yarn and knitting needles I sent. She has not begun using them for two reasons: she does not have an instruction book, and she wants more yarn so that she may knit a large men's sweater.

At her request, I had also included cod liver oil. She told me that she took it a couple of times and then somebody stole it. I felt disappointed. I am beginning to see for myself that she really cannot have anything of value at the boarding home. Thoughts of, "she should be living here with us," came to my mind. However, I know she is happy there. The thought of never sending anything there again also came to my mind.

After this phone call, I ended up sending her a couple of instruction books, so that she may get started knitting something. I did not send more yarn for a men's sweater. I wanted to know she was using the yarn I already sent before sending more.

I felt a bit guilty for not sending the additional yarn she had asked for, but I was just not convinced that if I sent more that she would actually use it.

December 1, 2018

Just thinking about my mother and wondering what I would do if her boarding home or center called to say she needs someone to care of her. This brought a couple of questions to my mind. What if our only opportunity to bring her closer to us was after she can no longer care for herself.

What would we do?

Should we jump at the opportunity to bring our mother closer to us under those circumstances?

I am not going to attempt to answer these questions right now. I may have one response today and a different response tomorrow. I believe my mother's mental illness has controlled all of her decisions. Should that make these types of questions easier to answer?

Finding Mother: A Journey of Loss and Love

January 23, 2019

I am thinking about the last conversation I had with my mother. I had not talked to her in a few weeks. Normally I would call every other week or so, but it had been around four weeks or more since I called. More time had gone by than usual. Well anyway, I called, she came to the phone, and she seemed happy to hear from me.

The first thing she said was, "I received the box you sent me."

Actually, she had already told me she received the box the last time we spoke. I had sent it before Christmas and we had already discussed it. She had already told me she liked everything I sent. I did not tell her we had already had that conversation.

We began to talk.

"Have you talked to Carla?" she asked.

I told her, "No, I have not talked to Carla. We still don't know where she is."

She inquired, "Have you talked to Terrance?"

"No. I have not."

She always asks about Carla and Terrance. My response is usually the same.

I asked, "How is your hip doing?"

"It feels uncomfortable, but it feels better since I got that shot to help with the pain. I still have to go to the doctor."

I felt like if she were in Kansas City, we would have taken her to the doctor for her hip a long time ago. It seems like she is very cooperative with the services provided by the center.

This is the phone call when she reminded me Valentine's Day was coming up. I guess if you grew up with my grandmother, as she did, you are going to enjoy those special days. Grandmother always observed special occasions.

She celebrated moments that were not holidays, too. Like, when she would bring me milkshakes at bedtime. Around the winter holidays, Grandmother would put up a tree, buy presents, bake cookies, and sing holiday songs. Grandmother was just a wonderful person. I could see why my mother would look forward to special occasions.

After we talked for a bit, she told me that the office worker was indicating to her that somebody else needed to use the phone.

I said, "Okay."

She said, "Thank you for calling. I like hearing your voice."

I said, "Thank you. I will try to call sooner next time."

She said, "Okay."

She did not seem like she really cared about how long it took me to call. She seemed like she was just happy that I had called when I did.

January 23, 2019

Just reminiscing about our very first reunion visit, when I asked my mother if she wanted me to find the children she had after she left us, and she said, "Yes."

I used the information she gave me to search for them. I even located a couple of people who I thought could actually be my siblings. After an unfavorable experience, I gave up searching for my siblings, at least for now.

Besides, I am still toiling concerning my relationship with my mother. Should I take on the responsibility of bringing new long-lost family into the equation at this time?

April 20, 2019

Today I was discussing a psychological theory. I was talking about how if a person is poor, and lives in a community that is not poor, that person may have more stress than if he or she lived in a place where everybody is poor.

This reminded me of my mother because she prefers to stay in the poor area where she is, even though we have offered her an opportunity to live in a community that is not poor.

When my brothers and I found her, we offered her the opportunity to come live in Kansas City with us. We showed her a beautiful place where she could live and told her how we wanted to take care of her. She did not outright reject it, but she said no to it because she likes where she is.

According to the center director, my mother is surrounded by drugs every day. According to my mother, she is surrounded by people who constantly steal from her. She is afraid to walk around in her community for fear of harm. If she does not go get her food in time, another resident will take her plate of food and eat it.

Nevertheless, that is her home and she is content to live there.

We have offered to move her to a place where she would not be surrounded by drugs, where people would not steal from her, where she would not have live in fear. She declined because she felt that what we were offering her was "luxury" and that she is not ready for anything like that right now.

She said, "I am used to where I am at. I kind of like it here."

Based on her response to our offer, I feel she may not be comfortable living in a community that was not poor.

Besides, sometimes I wonder: Would she still feel like she needs to carry her backpack around, to protect all of her belongings, even if she were in a place where nobody would steal from her?

Well anyway, we decided to let it go and not try to convince her to come away from the place where she is comfortable. If she is happy living there, then we are happy for her.

April 20, 2019

I was talking to my mother today. She was asleep, they woke her up, she sounded tired, but she came to the phone. She said that her hip had been giving her more trouble than usual. She said she saw the doctor at the center and they gave her some medication that makes her tired and sleepy. I guess that was why she was sleeping so well.

I asked her if she needed anything.

She said she needed some cigarettes.

When I was there, one of the boarding home workers had told me her favorite kind of cigarettes, and they were not very expensive. I actually thought cigarettes cost a lot more than that nowadays. At that price, my brothers and I had bought her a whole case of them while we were there.

While we were on the phone, I told her I already knew her favorite cigarettes since we bought them for her when we were there. She told me those cigarettes were not actually her favorite, but that her favorites were an expensive name brand cigarette; and that was what she wanted. She said she only smoked the more affordable cigarettes because she did not have the money to buy her favorite brand.

I actually feel guilty about the idea of sending cigarettes, let alone the most expensive ones, because I do not believe they are good for her health. I did not say that to her because I did not feel like I knew her well enough, and I did not want to come off as being judgmental.

I don't know.

Should I have just said it anyway?

Nevertheless, as I was preparing to send them, I found out it was against the law to send tobacco through the mail. I decided I would just send money instead. However, there are challenges to sending money because she does not have any way of cashing a check or a money order. The only option is to risk sending cash.

I wish there was some other way to get money to her.

April 28, 2019

On this day, I learned that my mother actually knows how to initiate a phone call to me. I have mixed feelings about it because she never calls me. I always initiate the phone calls to her and sometimes she does not come to the phone and does not return my calls. When she does come to the phone, she finds a reason to get off.

Today was different.

I had sent her some money, in lieu of cigarettes, and she did not receive it. She actually initiated a phone call to me, even though I had not called her first and even though the workers at her boarding home did not encourage her to make the call. She was calling because she had not received the money that I sent.

She called two times in a row but my phone was on silent and I did not get the calls. I realized she called when I saw the boarding home phone number on my list of missed calls and heard her talking on my voicemail.

She had never called me before.

I was not sure if I should be happy because she finally called me, or sad because she only called because she had not received the money.

May 12, 2019

I am still feeling discouraged about the cash I sent last month never arriving, so I did not send a Mother's Day card for fear it would not reach her.

Instead, I called my mother today to tell her Happy Mother's Day, but the phone just rang and no one answered. I tried a few more times this evening, but still no answer.

May 13, 2019

I called my mother again today because I did not want her to feel like I skipped acknowledging her for Mother's Day.

The boarding home worker who answered the phone told me she was not going to come to the phone, and did not bother with going to get her.

I have not heard from her anymore since the cash I sent got lost in the mail. I have tried calling her since then, but she did not come to the phone. Therefore, after today, I may not be calling or sending anything for a while.

June 16, 2019

    I called Mother today. The boarding home worker told me that she was in her room and that she was not going to come to the phone. That is the same thing the worker told me the last time I called about a month ago. The time before that, my mother chose not to come to the phone.

    This is the third time in a row that I called and have not been able to speak with her. I am not sure if it is her choice or if the worker just does not feel like going to get her to come to the phone.

    I feel sad about it, but it is okay.

    At least I found her and I know where she is.

August 6, 2019

I am still toiling about whether or not it is best, for my mother, if I continue to initiate communication with her. Nevertheless, I went on and sent her a care package. I called to let her know the package should have arrived, and spoke to her only briefly.

She said she would ask about it.

I called the next day to ensure she received it.

When I called this time, I told the boarding home worker I do not need to speak to her. I just wanted to confirm she received the package.

The worker jokingly said, "She would just think of a reason to get off the phone anyway."

I said, "Yeah."

We both laughed about it.

In reality, that truth was very hurtful for me.

The worker went and asked her, then came back to the phone to confirm that my mother had received it.

I said, "thank you," and we ended the call.

September 15, 2019

The last time I called the boarding home was when I called to confirm with my mother that she received the care package. I do not feel I should call her anymore.

I will continue to acknowledge her for special occasions. However, I think it is best for me, and for her, if I discontinue the phone calls.

She has been on her own for so many years and I think she is happy that way. Her actions have shown me four things:

That she appreciates our interest.

That she likes receiving gifts and money, mostly money.

That she prefers to be to herself.

That maybe she would be more content without the phone calls.

When she abandoned me when I was only two years old, I said to my grandmother, "Well if she don't want me, I don't want her *needer*." Today I say, "Well, if she don't want to talk to me, I don't want to talk to her *needer*." Overall, if she prefers to be to herself, then I will respect that.

I will always be grateful that I found her and happy that I know where she is.

September 22, 2019

I sent my mother a small package just to acknowledge her. I did not call her to let her know to look out for it the way I normally would. I just sent it and tried not worry about it. I really wanted to know if it was placed in her hands.

It is hard to send things without calling because I like to let her know to expect it. I also like to confirm she received it.

But, whenever I call, I have to contend with her either not coming to the phone, not calling me back, or acting like she needs to get off the phone; although, I am always more than willing to let her go as soon as I discuss the package I sent.

Calling her is uncomfortable because I feel like she would be content without me calling her. I know she likes receiving things, but there are challenges to me sending packages.

Besides the risk of it getting lost in the mail, it causes her to have to carry even more items around in her already heavy backpack. If she stores it in her bedroom, it will be stolen.

Therefore, I have every reason to stop calling and to stop sending things.

September 24, 2019

I ended up calling my mother this evening. I called to let her know the small package should have been delivered to her by now and to see if she had received it.

Here is how the call went:

The boarding home worker called her to the phone and she actually came! As she was picking up the phone to begin talking to me, I heard the boarding home worker say, "You only have two minutes, other people need to use the phone. This is a business phone."

I know from my own personal experience with the boarding home, that their phone hardly ever rings.

Was there really someone else who wanted to use the phone?

Was the worker serious about the phone being only for business, and not for personal calls?

Was the worker helping Geneva to be able to make a clean exit from our phone call?

Well, whatever the case, my mother sounded vibrant and happy to hear from me. I told her I heard what the boarding home worker said, so I would not keep her on the phone for a long time. I told her I sent her a package and just wanted to see if she had received it.

She seemed very interested and asked me to confirm the address I mailed it to. She said she had not received it, but she would be sure to check on it the next day.

I told her it would be nice if she could call me the next day to let me know, but that she did not have to.

She began asking questions about how my day was going and what I had been doing. I answered, then, in turn, I asked her how she had been doing. She sounded like she was really enjoying me and that she was happy I called.

I was feeling confused because of what I heard the boarding home worker say. I answered her questions very briefly and tried not to engage her in too much more conversation.

During this call, my mother said, "You know that last package you sent me?"

I said, "Yes."

She said, "My roommate stole it!"

I said, "That is horrible!" I saw it as a care package gone down the drain, but I could not blame anybody but myself. I knew the type of environment she lived in when I sent it.

This became the deciding factor that I absolutely will not be sending my mother any more packages.

She did not call the next day to let me know if she received the current package, so I did not call her either.

I figured either she got it or she didn't.

IN CLOSING...

As far as calling and sending things are concerned: I have resolved to simply sending a small card with a very, very small amount of cash inside, only on special occasions. I will refrain from calling to confirm if she has received it.

If the amount I send is small enough, then I will not need to worry myself about whether she received it.

If I stop sending packages, then I can stop worrying about them getting lost in the mail, or being stolen by her roommates, and I will not need to call to confirm whether she received the things.

If she ever wants to talk to me, she can call because she has my phone number.

So many times, people see reunions like ours and assume things were happily ever after. They never find out what *really* happened after the reunion. The questions, the challenges, the toiling. In spite of all of that, I would find my mother again, and again, and again.

These emotions, thoughts and feelings I have experienced are nothing compared to actually finding my mother.

Finding Mother: A Journey of Loss and Love

Discussion Contents

Book One - Discussion Questions
Book One - Questions Teachers Can Ask
Book One - Further Discussion Points

Book Two - Discussion Questions
Book Two - Questions Teachers Can Ask
Book Two - Further Discussion Points

Book Three - Discussion Questions
Book Three - Questions Teachers Can Ask
Book Three - Further Discussion Points

Book Four - Discussion Questions
Book Four - Questions Teachers Can Ask
Book Four - Further Discussion Points

Book One - Discussion Questions

1. Name some mental illness behaviors that Mother exhibited before she left her family.

2. Name some ways Father coped with Mother's mental illness. Discuss your response.

3. Growing up, the author felt like Father was the cause of Mother's mental illness becoming more intense. Discuss why you agree or disagree.

4. Do you think it is possible to "knock sense into" a mentally ill person? Why or Why not?

5. Do you think Mother's running away could have been prevented? If so, how? If not, why not?

6. The author specifically remembers being physically harmed by her mother, but still wanted to find her and take care of her. What are your thoughts about that?

Finding Mother: A Journey of Loss and Love

Book One -Questions Teachers Can Ask
Critical Thinking/In-depth Comprehension/Writing Skills/Technology Skills

1. What is the main idea or learning experience of the book?

2. Summarize your favorite part of the book and tell why this was your favorite part.

3. Write about an experience in your personal life and tell how it is similar to this story.

4. Write a summary of the story, highlighting what you think the main issues are.

5. To whom would you recommend this book? Why?

6. How can the information in the story be useful in your life or future?

7. Research a famous or infamous person on the computer who was abandoned by their mother, and write a report about that person's life.

8. Research a famous or infamous person on the computer who suffered from a mental illness, and write a report about that person's life.

Book One - Further Discussion Points

Finding Mother after Five Decades indicated some of Geneva's Symptoms and Coping Behaviors for her mental illness. Below are some excerpts from the book that you may use for additional discussion.

Symptoms

Unable to perform Daily Activities. According to the author's father, Geneva was unable to work, cook, clean house, or dress properly. Read and discuss the excerpt below.

I believe my father experienced a lot of stress and disappointment due to my mother having a mental illness and not being able to provide him with the support he desired from a wife. She was unable to work, cook meals, or clean the house the way my father expected her to.

Child Abuse. In addition to stories from family members, the author remembers being harmed physically by Geneva. Read and discuss the excerpts below.

I heard stories about my mother's mental illness causing her to experience episodes, which resulted in her harming my siblings and me.

He explained to me that my father usually physically harmed her because she physically harmed us.

Then, to come home after a very long, tedious work day and find no dinner ready, the house dirty, or her having harmed one of the children, was an even heavier burden.

Coping Behaviors

Denial. It appears Geneva may have been in denial about having children for all of the years she has been gone. Read and discuss the excerpt below.

April said it sounded like we were talking about the same Geneva, but she said Geneva never said anything about having children. "I had always wondered if she had children," April said. "She always acted evasive whenever the subject would come up." She continued, "This all makes sense now."

These *Further Discussion Points* are only a few things that stood out for the author from her own story. Did you see any additional Symptoms or Coping Behaviors as you read the book? If so, please free to discuss them.

Book Two - Discussion Questions

1. Name at least three (3) common symptoms of Mother's diagnosis.

2. Did Mother exhibit any of these symptoms? If so, which ones?

3. Discuss the difference between an assisted living facility and a nursing home.

4. What are your thoughts about the author's phone conversations with Mother.

5. The author thought Mother's center was a place that merely provided fun activities. What was it instead? What, if any, thoughts do you have about that?

6. Why do you think the center manager allowed Geneva to skip the center activities and talk with the author and Arica instead?

7. Mother never wanted more than two children. She ended up having ten and left them all. Do you think Mother would have still run away if she had only had the two children she desired? Why or why not? Discuss your response.

8. Mother told Arica how she felt when the author and her brothers first showed up to reunite with her. What are your thoughts about how Mother felt?

9. Discuss why you think mother changed her mind about going out to eat with the author?

10. Name three (3) ways the author showed "Acceptance."

Book Two - Questions Teachers Can Ask
Critical Thinking/In-depth Comprehension/Writing Skills/Technology Skills

1. What is the main idea or learning experience of the book?
2. Write your thoughts or feelings about the story or your favorite character.
3. Summarize your favorite part of the book and tell why this was your favorite part.
4. Write about an experience in your personal life and tell how it is similar to this story.
5. Write a summary of the story, highlighting what you think the main issues are.
6. To whom would you recommend this book? Why?
7. How can the information in the story be useful in your life or future?
8. Research a famous or infamous person on the computer who has had a similar experience, and write a report about that person's life.

Book Two - Further Discussion Points

After the Reunion indicated some of Geneva's Symptoms, Coping Behaviors, and Treatments for her mental illness. It also indicated some Effects this has had on the author. Below are some excerpts, from the book, that you may use for additional discussion.

Symptoms

Hallucinations. One symptom of Geneva's diagnosis is hallucinations. She often referred to the things she was hearing from "people upstairs on the third floor." Geneva seemed to be having *auditory* hallucinations. Read and discuss the excerpts below.

However, whenever the subject came up of why she left our family, she would either start talking about something else, or tell me about the things she was hearing from the "people on the third floor."
Note: this could also be avoidance.

I believe the "people upstairs" were actually voices she was hearing in her head. However, she did not perceive the voices as being in her head. She believed they were in the same house with her, but on a different floor in the boarding home.

She said, "No, the people upstairs told him that."

Accepting the fact that I may never get her full story without her referring to the people on the "third floor."
Note: this could also be avoidance.

Coping Behaviors

Denial. When the author and her siblings went to reunite with Geneva, she denied them at first, then later accepted them. Read and discuss the excerpt below.

During our reunion visit, I noted that the more she looked at the pictures, the more it began to "click" for her that we were her

Finding Mother: A Journey of Loss and Love

children. The more she realized we were her children, the more she opened up, and eventually accepted us. To say that the pictures were a powerful tool would be an understatement.

Denial. Geneva had been in denial about having children for all of the years the she has been gone. The boarding home workers, center manager, her counselor, NOBODY knew she had children when the author and her siblings went to reunite and visit with her. Therefore, she had kept this secret to herself for almost 50 years! Read and discuss the excerpts below.

I told her I was Geneva's daughter and that my siblings and I had found her after forty-nine years. She expressed a variety of feelings. "Oh my, I am so excited that the two of you are here! This is a surprise! I never even knew Geneva had children!

I felt embarrassed for my mother because I knew she had been living in denial about having children for forty-nine years. I knew she had not revealed to anyone that she had children.

The woman said, "Geneva, I didn't know you had children!" Geneva just stared ahead with a blank look on her face and did not respond.

I wondered if she had been in denial as a way of burying the emotional pain and embarrassment of having left us so many years ago.

Everyone who I met at the boarding home acted shocked about Geneva having children. Some of them had known her for over fifteen years, and they never had a clue she had given birth.

Guilt. The author believed that Geneva was feeling guilty for abandoning them. Read and discuss the excerpt below.

I believed she may have been experiencing a lot of guilt for not wanting her children.

Finding Mother: A Journey of Loss and Love

Avoidance. Geneva said, on several occasions, that she had "business" to take care of before she could reunite, move closer, move forward with her relationship with the author and her siblings. Read and discuss the excerpts below.

When I asked her if I could help her take care of her business, she said she could do it herself.

Eventually, I began to wonder if she really had "business," or if she was just trying to protect my feelings because she did not know how to tell me that moving closer to us, and allowing us to take care of her, was never in her plans.

Avoidance. Whenever the author tried to talk about something Geneva was not comfortable talking about, Geneva would start talking about the people "upstairs" on the "third floor" even though there was no third floor in the boarding home. Read and discuss the excerpts below.

She started talking about the people upstairs on the "third floor" again. From my time with my mother, she usually starts reverting to the "third floor" to avoid dealing with the reality of painful memories.

"I feel like I pretty much know the details surrounding why you left, but I just need to hear it from you." Again, she reverted to talking about the voices from "upstairs."

"Were you in a mental hospital at the time of my birth?" She said, "Yes." I told her, "I thought maybe that was the case, and maybe that was why you were not able to take me home." She mentioned the people "upstairs" again.

Treatments. Treatment for Geneva has included:
- **Medication**
- **Psychosocial Intervention**
- **Hospitalization**

Finding Mother: A Journey of Loss and Love

Medication. The mental illness that Geneva has affects her actions, thoughts and feelings. It causes her to see the world differently from someone who does not have a mental illness. This means she may try to avoid taking her medication. Sometimes it may be challenging to get her to cooperate. Read and discuss the excerpts below.

The staff came up with a bright idea to check under the mattress on her bed. There they found the pills she was supposed to be taking daily, but she had been hiding them instead.

I told her that some of the benefits were weekly housekeeping, laundry service, three meals a day, and medication management. "The nurses come to your room to assist you with taking your medication." Mother seemed a little nervous when I mentioned the medication part.

All of a sudden, I heard someone shout, "Medication!" It was a worker in the office. This was a call for all residents to come over to the office door, stand in line and take their medication.

Psychosocial Interventions. Geneva receives this type of treatment through the boarding home where she lives and the mental health treatment center where she attends daily. Between the two programs, she is able to manage her mental illness and live somewhat of an independent lifestyle. Read and discuss the excerpts below.

She explained to me that Geneva resided in an assisted living facility, in which they cook, clean, wash clothes, and manage medication for the residents.

The work of the center includes evaluating mental health patients, setting behavior goals, creating treatment plans and providing therapeutic activities. While there, Mother participates with group counseling, games and trips to the park. She also receives lunch and a snack and learns life skills.

Overall, I was impressed with the work of the boarding home and mental health treatment center. I realized they are committed to that specific community of people. They have taken on the challenge of providing their basic physical, emotional and mental health needs.

Psychosocial Intervention: Social Support. During the author's second trip to visit Geneva, the mental health treatment center allowed her to sit in the lobby and talk with the author in lieu of center activities. Read and discuss the excerpt below.

For a moment, I was feeling a little guilt, like we were causing her to miss the center activities. Then I realized the staff probably felt like visiting with her long-lost family may be more therapeutic to her than participating with the center for that day.

Mental Hospital. During times when symptoms are severe, patients may be hospitalized to help relieve symptoms. The author's story indicates that Geneva has been a mental hospital patient numerous times throughout her life. Read and discuss the excerpts below.

Donna said she had to remind my mother that if she did not take her medication that she could end up locked up in a mental hospital again. Having a fear of going back there, she started taking it regularly.

However, if she refuses to take it, her uncontrollable behavior places her at risk of being committed, against her will, to a mental hospital.

From her story, coupled with things I already knew, I gathered that she had already been in and out of mental facilities several times before I was even born."
It was in Kansas City where she experienced her final mental hospital stay before leaving our family for good.

They told me it was a regular hospital, that would help my body rejuvenate and give me some rest from the kids. After they admitted me, I found out it was a mental hospital.

Finding Mother: A Journey of Loss and Love

She recalled being in the mental hospital and no one ever coming to see her. 'He stayed away.

She alleged, "There is a lot I don't know. I did not have a chance to talk to my husband before I left the mental hospital with a friend.

"Were you in a mental hospital at the time of my birth?" She said, "Yes."

Effects on the author

Feeling Emotional. After the very emotional reunion, the author needed to talk about her thoughts and feeling with someone who would listen to her, and not be judgmental. Read and discuss the excerpts below.

After a meticulous online search, I found the number of a counseling hotline where I could speak with someone freely without revealing my true identity[...]Realizing I finally had a golden opportunity to share what was on my heart concerning my mother, with someone who did not know me and therefore could not judge me, tears welled up in my eyes. I cried and began to talk about my feelings.

These *Further Discussion Points* are only a few things that stood out for the author from her own story. Did you see any additional Symptoms, Coping Behaviors, Treatments or Effects on the author as you read the book? If so, please free to discuss them.

Finding Mother: A Journey of Loss and Love

Book Three - Discussion Questions

1. Mother talked to the author and Jerome on the phone before they traveled to reunite with her. What reason(s) did she express for not accepting them as her children upon their arrival?

2. What did the author do to try to get Mother to accept them during the very first attempt?

3. What, if anything, could they have done differently to cause Mother to accept them during their first attempt? Discuss your response.

4. The author and her brothers felt rejected and discouraged after the first meeting, but they returned the next day to try again. If you were in their situation, would you have tried to reunite for a second time? Or would you have just gone back home? Discuss your response.

5. Name one or more things the author did to get Mother to finally receive them when they went back the second time.

6. During the second attempt to win over Mother, the author did not give up until Mother agreed to reunite with the brothers. What are your thoughts about this?

7. The author and her brothers offered their mother a "better life" with them in Kansas City. What was Mother's response?

   What are your thoughts about Mother response?

8. Why do you think the author called this book a "Story of Tenacity?"

Book Three - Questions Teachers Can Ask
Critical Thinking/In-depth Comprehension/Writing Skills/Technology Skills

1. What is the main idea or learning experience of the book?

2. Write your thoughts or feelings about the story or your favorite character.

3. Summarize your favorite part of the book and tell why this was your favorite part.

4. Write about an experience in your personal life and tell how it is similar to this story.

5. Write a summary of the story, highlighting what you think the main issues are.

6. To whom would you recommend this book? Why?

7. How can the information in the story be useful in your life or future?

8. Research a famous or infamous person on the computer who was abandoned by their mother, and write a report about that person's life.

9. Research a famous or infamous person on the computer who suffered from a mental illness, and write a report about that person's life.

Book Three - Further Discussion Points

Reuniting with Mother indicated some of Geneva's Symptoms, Coping Behaviors, and Treatments for her mental illness. It also indicated some Effects this has had on the author. Below are some excerpts, from the book, that you may use for additional discussion.

Symptoms

Hallucinations. One symptom of Geneva's diagnosis is hallucinations. She often referred to the things she was hearing from "people upstairs on the third floor." Geneva seemed to be having *auditory* hallucinations. Read and discuss the excerpts below.

She began telling me about the people upstairs on "the third floor" who have been saying that her "husband" was still alive.

Furthermore, I knew that there was no "third floor" in the boarding home, so I presumed she was referring to the voices she hears in her head due to having a mental illness.

Abandonment. Geneva only wanted two children, but had a total of ten, and left them all. Read and discuss the excerpts below.

She mentioned again that she had ten children and told me she initially only wanted two children, a boy and a girl. She said, "If anybody would have told me I was going to have ten children, I would not have believed them!"

At that moment, I remembered how my father would rant about how she did not want all of the children she was having. Yet, she did not believe in birth control or abortion. Hearing her say she never wanted so many children caused me to think about the adverse effect it must have had on her mental illness.

Coping Behaviors

Denial. When the author and her siblings went to reunite with Geneva, she denied them at first, then, later accepted them. Read and discuss the excerpts below.

She looked at each of us again, and just when it appeared she might actually accept us as her children, she said, "You are not my people. Anybody can come in here and say they are my people."

"You all are strangers. I don't talk to strangers about anything personal. I'm not giving out any information unless I know who I am talking to."

We assured her she did not owe us anything, that we were not looking for any apologies, that we loved her and just wanted to see her. She said, "No, I don't trust that,"

Denial. It appears Geneva may have been in denial about having children for all of the years she had been gone. Read and discuss the excerpt below.

But, she walked into the dining room with an extremely surprised look on her face. She looked at Geneva and said, "You never told me anything about having children! I had no idea!" Geneva looked at her but did not say anything. The worker left the room and we continued to eat.

Denial. The author's sister was in denial about having a mental illness, therefore was not taking medication for major symptoms. Therefore, her siblings were not able to take her with them when they went to reunite with their mother. Read and discuss the excerpt below.

You see, we really wanted to take her with us but she has the same mental illness as my mother. However, she was in denial about it and not taking medication to manage it. We were afraid that if we took her with us, we would not be equipped to care for her if she were to have an episode.

Finding Mother: A Journey of Loss and Love

Avoidance. Geneva said, on several occasions, that she had "business" to take care of before she could reunite, move closer, or move forward with her relationship with the author and her siblings. Read and discuss the excerpts below.

Then, her face looked less afraid and she said, "Ok." I became excited and asked her which one of her sons she wanted to reunite with first. She said, "Wait, not yet! I'm not ready. I have to take care of my business."

He told her that if she ever wants to leave there and come live in Kansas City with us, just call him and he would make it happen. She said she would let him know, but that she has a lot of business to take care of before she could consider moving.

Terrance told her that if she moved to Kansas City, it would be easy for us to take her to have her teeth fixed. We could monitor the process and take her to all of her appointments. She reminded him of the "business" she has to take care of before she could consider moving.

The feeling of gratefulness in my heart matched the tenaciousness of my mind. If, by chance, she really did have "business," I felt determined to find out what it was and help her with it.

Avoidance. Geneva often referred to the "people upstairs on the third floor" to avoid talking about events that were stressful for her. Read and discuss the excerpt below.

Therefore, instead of answering my question, she went back to talking about the people "upstairs."

Treatments. Treatment for Geneva has included:
- **Medication**
- **Psychosocial Intervention**
- **Hospitalization**

Medication. The mental illness that Geneva has affects her actions, thoughts and feelings. It causes her to see the world differently from someone who does not have a mental illness. This means she may try to avoid taking her medication. Sometimes it may be challenging to get her to cooperate. Read and discuss the excerpt below.

Ashley claimed that Geneva never talks to her and that she usually has a hard time getting her to take her medication, whereas April had given us a completely different account.

Psychosocial Interventions. Geneva receives this type of treatment through the boarding home where she lives and the mental health treatment center where she attends daily. Between the two programs, she is able to manage her mental illness and live somewhat of an independent lifestyle. Read and discuss the excerpt below.

Miss Adams took me to see Geneva's bedroom. She had a smile and a proud look on her face as she told me how she made up the bed and how she cleans my mother's room every day.

Effects on the author

Feeling Hurt. The author felt hurt after Geneva denied them.

Witnessing her living in a state of poverty and suffering from a mental illness helped me to understand why she left us. Nevertheless, it still hurt deeply. I had always blamed my father for her leaving, but after this failed reunion, I was placing all the blame on her.

These *Further Discussion Points* are only a few things that stood out for the author from her own story. Did you see any additional Symptoms, Coping Behaviors, Treatments or Effects on the author as you read the book? If so, please free to discuss them.

Book Four - Discussion Questions

1. Do you think Grace should keep calling and sending things to her mother? Why or why not?

2. Do you believe Grace has forgiven her mother for leaving her when she was two years old? Why or why not?

3. How does a mother just abandon her children and not want to be with them when they find her? Discuss your thoughts about this.

4. Do you think Mother will feel sad if Grace never calls again, even though she has Grace's phone number but never calls her? Discuss your response.

5. Do you think Grace would have had a happier life if her mentally ill mother would have never abandoned her?

6. Grace feels like her mother does not really want, or need, her in her life? Discuss your thoughts about this.

7. Grace's father expected her mother to do all the things he expected from a wife, even though she had a mental illness. What do you think about his expectations? Discuss your response.

8. What if Grace's only opportunity to bring her mother to live closer, was after her mother could no longer care for herself? Do you feel Grace should jump at the opportunity to bring her mother closer under those circumstances?

9. What are your thoughts about Grace's decision not to search for her other siblings at this time?

10. Grace felt guilty about sending her mother the cigarettes she asked for, because she believed they are not good for her health. She did not say that to her mother because she felt like she did not know her mother well enough and she did not want to come off as being judgmental. Should she have just said it anyway? Why or Why not?

Book Four - Questions Teachers Can Ask
Critical Thinking/In-depth Comprehension/Writing Skills/Technology Skills

1. What is the main idea or learning experience of the book?
2. Write your thoughts or feelings about the story.
3. Summarize your favorite part of the book and tell why this was your favorite part.
4. Write about an experience in your personal life and tell how it is similar to this story.
5. Write a new summary for the book.
6. To whom would you recommend this book? Why?
7. How can the information in the story be useful in your life or future?
8. Research a famous or infamous person on the computer who was abandoned by their mother, and write a report about that person's life.
9. Research a famous or infamous person on the computer who suffered from a mental illness, and write a report about that person's life.
10. Find a book in the library written by an author who has published their personal diary, and discuss how that book is different from this one.

Finding Mother: A Journey of Loss and Love

Book Four - Further Discussion Points

Diary of Emotions indicated some of the Effects this has had on the author. Below are some excerpts, from the book, that you may use for additional discussion about mental health.

Effects on the author

Motherly instincts took author by surprise. After being away from Geneva for so many years, the author felt surprised when Geneva showed motherly instincts. Read and discuss the excerpts below.

However, one time we were talking on the phone and I told her I was not feeling well. She immediately started giving me pointers about how to take care of myself, you know, like a mother would do. I just said, "Yeah," as if to tell her, "I already know how to take care of myself." I felt surprised that her motherly instinct actually stepped up in that moment. My first instinct was to feel like I did not need a mother. In a way, I felt honored that she showed that she cared. In another way, it felt unusual for her to act "motherly" towards me after being away for my entire life.

I called my mother today. When I told her today was my birthday, she sang the "Happy Birthday" song to me. I thought that was nice of her. She sang... "Happy birthday to you, happy birthday to you, happy birthday dear Grace, happy birthday to you." I could picture her with a wide smile on her face. I had never heard my own mother sing "Happy Birthday" to me in my entire life. I had assorted feelings throughout the song.

Feeling unwanted by her mother. While the author feels grateful for finding her mother, there are some things in her story that indicate she may, at times, feel unwanted by her mother. Read and discuss the excerpt below.

Still, I asked myself, "Is her hip really hurting that badly, or is this a sign that she still does not want me after all of these years?"

Finding Mother: A Journey of Loss and Love

I would hate for her to experience the same rejection from me that she experienced from my father. However, I am afraid I may approach another point in my life where I will have to say, "Well, if she don't want me, I don't want her needer."

I always initiate the phone calls to her and sometimes she does not come to the phone and does not return my phone call. When she does come to the phone, she finds a reason to get off.

These *Further Discussion Points* are only a few things that stood out for the author from her own story. Did you see any additional Effects on the author as you read the book? If so, please free to discuss them.

FINDING MOTHER SERIES

A Gifted Child in Foster Care:
A Story Resilience – REVISED EDITION
In this book, Dr. Grace LaJoy shares her life story of being deserted by her mother, living in foster care, and ending up in a gifted and talented class while still in foster care. She recalls her life story before, during and after foster care. The *Finding Mother Series* was written as a sequel to this book.

Finding Mother After Five Decades:
A Story of Hope
Grace LaJoy's determination pays off when she finally finds her mother who abandoned her at age two. Discover the specific details about her intriguing journey in **Finding Mother after Five Decades,** BOOK 1 of the *Finding Mother Series.*

Reuniting with Mother:
A Story of Tenacity
What happens when Grace LaJoy and her siblings come face-to-face with their estranged mother after 49 years? How does she receive them? Find out in **Reuniting with Mother,** BOOK 2 of the *Finding Mother Series.*

Finding Mother: A Journey of Loss and Love

After the Reunion:
A Story of Acceptance
After a very emotional reunion, Grace LaJoy has two concerns to address with her long-lost mother. What are her concerns? Does she get the answers she needs from her mother? Find out in **After the Reunion,** BOOK 3 of the *Finding Mother Series.*

Diary of Emotion:
Thoughts and Feelings
After reuniting with her mother after 49 years, Grace LaJoy toils with an array of thoughts and feeling. She reveals them all in **Diary of Emotions,** BOOK 4 of the *Finding Mother Series.*

Available in Paperback and Kindle eBook
Collect them all!
Ask for the series in
bookstores and libraries
www.gracelajoy.com

Author Grace LaJoy and her mother, "Geneva"

CPSIA information can be obtained
at www.ICGtesting.com
Printed in the USA
BVHW070735290121
599074BV00005B/1214